ULTIMATE MUSIC THEORY

By Glory St. Germain ARCT RMT MYCC UMTC &
Shelagh McKibbon-U'Ren RMT UMTC

Introducing the Ultimate Music Theory Family!

So-La

Ti-Do

Meet So-La! So-La loves to sing and dance.

She is expressive, creative and loves to tell stories through music!

So-La feels music in her heart. She loves to teach, compose and perform.

Meet Ti-Do! Ti-Do loves to count and march.

He is rhythmic, consistent and loves the rules of music theory!

Ti-Do feels music in his hands and feet. He loves to analyze, share tips and conduct.

So-La & Ti-Do will guide you through Mastering Music Theory!

Enriching Lives Through Music Education

ISBN: 978-1-927641-23-1

Ultimate Music Theory - *The Way to Score Success!*

The Ultimate Music Theory Beginner Series consists of 3 workbooks: A, B and C. These workbooks provide young students with a solid foundation in theory and piano pedagogy.

Teachers and Students are encouraged to play each theory lesson on the piano to develop and strengthen the connection between theory (what is seen) and piano (what is heard and played). These techniques will develop strong musicianship skills in Ear Training and Sight Reading.

At the end of each of the 12 lessons is an accumulative Review Test that reinforces all concepts learned from the very first Lesson. To support a stress-free learning environment, the Review Tests are not graded. Simply CHECK ✓ each **Review with So-La & Ti-Do** upon successful completion.

Published in 2018 by Gloryland Publishing
Printed in Canada.
GlorylandPublishing.com

Library and Archives Canada Cataloguing in Publication
Ultimate Music Theory Beginner A B C Series / Glory St. Germain and Shelagh McKibbon-U'Ren

Gloryland Publishing - Ultimate Music Theory Series:

GP - TBA	ISBN: 978-1-927641-21-7	Ultimate Music Theory Beginner Level A
GP - TBB	ISBN: 978-1-927641-22-4	Ultimate Music Theory Beginner Level B
GP - TBC	ISBN: 978-1-927641-23-1	Ultimate Music Theory Beginner Level C
GP - UP1	ISBN: 978-0-9809556-6-8	Ultimate Prep 1 Rudiments
GP - UP1A	ISBN: 978-0-9809556-9-9	Ultimate Prep 1 Rudiments Answer Book
GP - UP2	ISBN: 978-0-9809556-7-5	Ultimate Prep 2 Rudiments
GP - UP2A	ISBN: 978-0-9813101-0-7	Ultimate Prep 2 Rudiments Answer Book
GP- UBR	ISBN: 978-0-9813101-3-8	Ultimate Basic Rudiments
GP - UBRA	ISBN: 978-0-9813101-4-5	Ultimate Basic Answer Book
GP - UIR	ISBN: 978-0-9813101-5-2	Ultimate Intermediate Rudiments
GP - UIRA	ISBN: 978-0-9813101-6-9	Ultimate Intermediate Answer Book
GP - UAR	ISBN: 978-0-9813101-7-6	Ultimate Advanced Rudiments
GP - UARA	ISBN: 978-0-9813101-8-3	Ultimate Advanced Answer Book
GP - UCR	ISBN: 978-0-9813101-1-4	Ultimate Complete Rudiments
GP - UCRA	ISBN: 978-0-9813101-2-1	Ultimate Complete Answer Book

♫ **Note:** The Ultimate Music Theory Program includes the UMT Workbook Series, Exam Series and Supplemental Series to help students successfully prepare for national theory exams.

UltimateMusicTheory.com

Music Theory Beginner C

So-La

Ti-Do

Table of Contents

Ultimate Music Theory Guide & Chart - Beginner C

Ultimate Music Theory - *The Way to Score Success!*

Lesson 1 Keyboard - Same, Step, Skip, Leap & Octave

KEYBOARD - MUSICAL ALPHABET - LOW, MIDDLE and HIGH SOUNDS

The WHITE keys repeat the 7 letter names of the Musical Alphabet over and over.
Each key has a different pitch. The PITCH is how LOW or HIGH a note sounds.

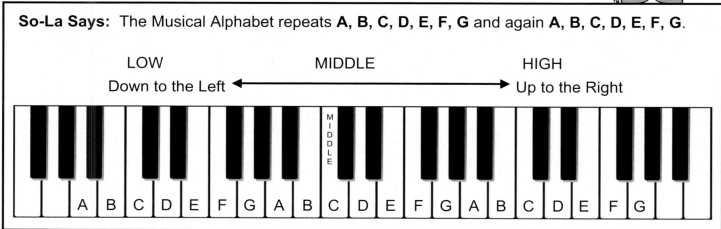

So-La Says: The Musical Alphabet repeats **A, B, C, D, E, F, G** and again **A, B, C, D, E, F, G**.

♫ **Ti-Do Tip:** When moving from left to right UP the keyboard, the sound gets HIGHER in pitch.

1. Write the Musical Alphabet A, B, C, D, E, F, G going UP the keyboard - Low to Middle to High.

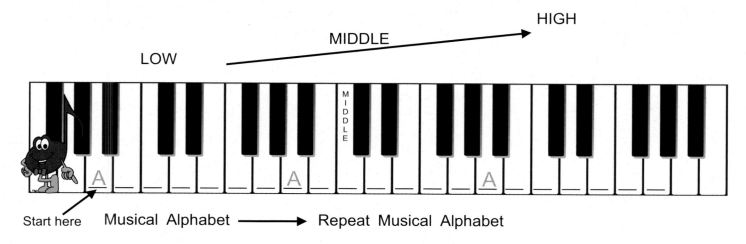

Start here   Musical Alphabet ———→ Repeat Musical Alphabet

♫ **Ti-Do Tip:** When moving from right to left DOWN the keyboard, the sound gets LOWER in pitch.

2. Write the Musical Alphabet G, F, E, D, C, B, A going DOWN the keyboard - High to Middle to Low.

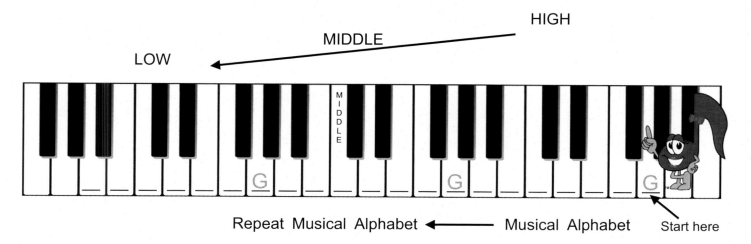

Repeat Musical Alphabet ←——— Musical Alphabet   Start here

WHITE KEYS - PATTERN, DISTANCE and INTERVAL

So-La Says: Notes have a Pattern, Distance and Interval.

A PATTERN can be the Same (repeated note) or move up or down by a Step, Skip, Leap or an Octave.

The DISTANCE is each note counted in the pattern.

An INTERVAL is the number (distance between notes).

Pattern	Distance	Interval
Same	First	1
Step	Second	2
Skip	Third	3
Leap	Fifth	5
Octave	Eighth	8

Distance: first   second   third   fifth   eighth

| 1 A | 1 C | 2 D | 1 F | 2 | 3 A | 1 C | 2 | 3 | 4 | 5 G | 1 B | 2 | 3 | 4 | 5 | 6 | 7 | 8 B |

Pattern: same   step   skip   leap   octave

Interval: 1   2   3   5   8

1. Fill in the blanks. Name the Distance and Interval Number for each Pattern.

    Pattern: Same is counted as the Distance of a _____, Interval ___.

    Pattern: Step is counted as the Distance of a _____, Interval ___.

    Pattern: Skip is counted as the Distance of a _____, Interval ___.

    Pattern: Leap is counted as the Distance of a _____, Interval ___.

    Pattern: Octave is counted as the Distance of an _____, Interval ___.

2. For the given keys on the keyboard, name the Pattern and Interval for each Distance.

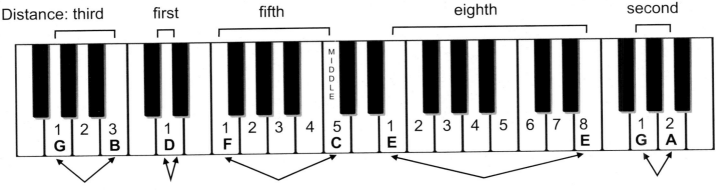

Distance: third   first   fifth   eighth   second

| 1 G | 2 | 3 B | 1 D | 1 F | 2 | 3 | 4 | 5 C | 1 E | 2 | 3 | 4 | 5 | 6 | 7 | 8 E | 1 G | 2 A |

Pattern: _____ _____   _____   _____   _____

Interval: ___   ___   ___   ___   ___

WHITE KEYS - COUNTING INTERVALS - SAME (FIRST), STEP (SECOND) and SKIP (THIRD)

So-La Says: When naming Distances (Intervals) of a same (first), step (second) or skip (third), count from the left (lower key) going UP to the right (higher key) on the keyboard.

The first key (given note) is counted as 1. Count each key.

Distance:	first	third	second	third	third	second	first

Pattern:	same	skip	step	skip	skip	step	same
Interval:	1	3	2	3	3	2	1

♫ **Ti-Do Tip:** Intervals count UP the Musical Alphabet (left to right) on the keyboard.
→ Same - A repeat A (1); Step - A, B (1, 2); Skip - A, B, C (1, 2, 3)

1. Step up a second from each given key. Name the key on the keyboard. Name the Interval.

Interval: ___   ___   ___   ___   ___   ___   ___

2. Skip up a third from each given key. Name the key on the keyboard. Name the Interval.

Interval: ___   ___   ___   ___   ___   ___   ___

WHITE KEYS - COUNTING INTERVALS - LEAP (FIFTH) and OCTAVE (EIGHTH)

So-La Says: When naming Distances (Intervals) of a leap (fifth) or eighth (octave), count from the left (lower key) going UP to the right (higher key) on the keyboard.

The first key (given note) is counted as 1. Count each key.

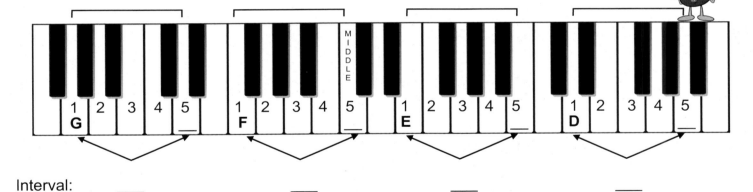

Distance: fifth   eighth   fifth   eighth

Pattern: leap   octave   leap   octave

Interval: 5   8   5   8

♫ **Ti-Do Tip:** Intervals count UP the Musical Alphabet (left to right) on the keyboard.
→ Leap - A, B, C, D, E (1, 2, 3, 4, 5); Octave - A, B, C, D, E, F, G, A (1, 2, 3, 4, 5, 6, 7, 8)

1. Leap up a fifth from each given key. Name the key on the keyboard. Name the Interval.

Interval: ___   ___   ___   ___

2. Octave up an eighth from each given key. Name the key on the keyboard. Name the Interval.

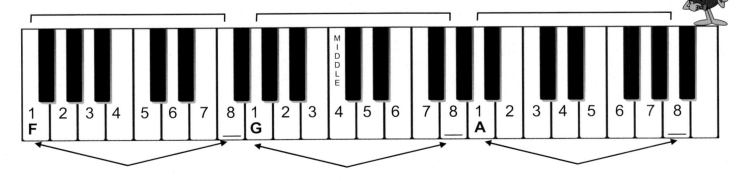

Interval: ___   ___   ___

Lesson 1 Review with So-La & Ti-Do

Check:

1. For the Distance below each bracket:
   WRITE the Numbers to count each key (1, 2, 3, etc.) directly on the keyboard.
   WRITE the Letter Name of each key (A, B, C, etc.).
   WRITE the Pattern (same, step, skip, leap or octave).
   WRITE the Interval Number (1, 2, 3, 5 or 8).

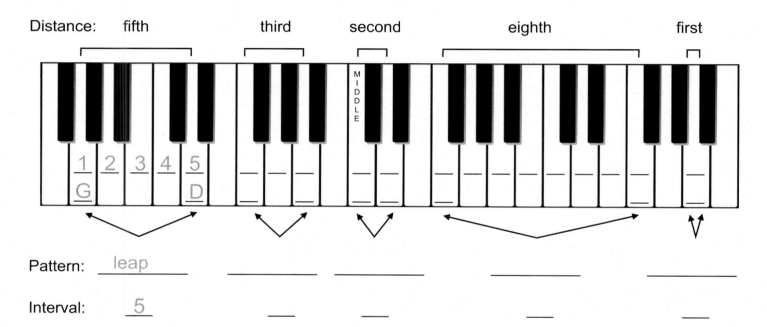

Distance: fifth   third   second   eighth   first

Pattern: ___leap___   _____   _____   _____   _____

Interval: 5   ___   ___   ___   ___

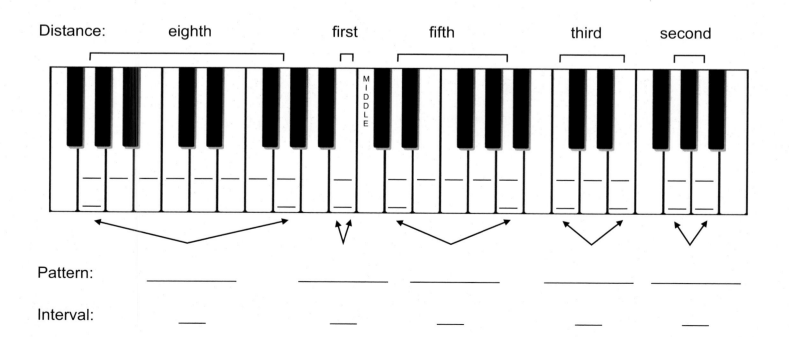

Distance: eighth   first   fifth   third   second

Pattern: _____   _____   _____   _____   _____

Interval: ___   ___   ___   ___   ___

Lesson 1 Review Ultimate Sight Reading & Ear Training Games

1. PLAY each Interval on the piano.
   WRITE the correct Distance above each Interval (first, second, third, fifth or eighth).

   LISTEN as your Teacher plays one of the Intervals. Is your Teacher playing the Interval that is close together or far apart? Color the correct Balloon.

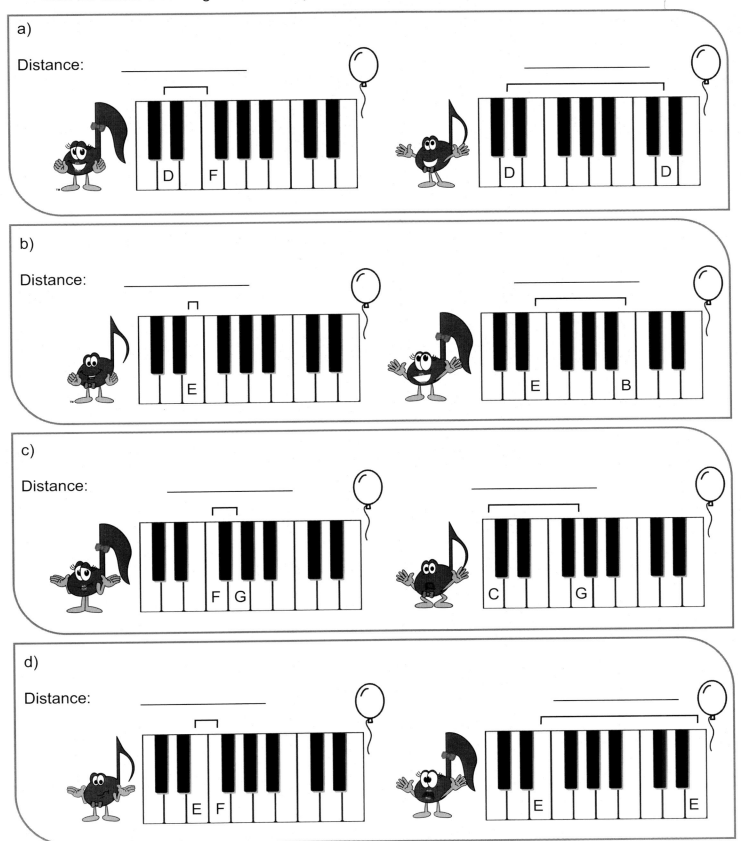

Lesson 2   Treble Clef and Bass Clef - Lines, Spaces and Patterns

TREBLE CLEF - 5 LINES (E, G, B, D, F) and 4 SPACES (F, A, C, E)

The **TREBLE CLEF** or **G CLEF** is drawn on the STAFF. Music notes written in the Treble Clef (or Treble Staff) are drawn as a circle (oval shape) called a Whole Note.

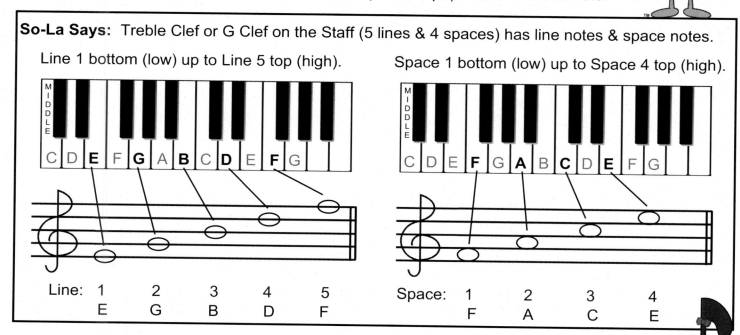

So-La Says: Treble Clef or G Clef on the Staff (5 lines & 4 spaces) has line notes & space notes.

Line 1 bottom (low) up to Line 5 top (high).

Space 1 bottom (low) up to Space 4 top (high).

Line:	1	2	3	4	5
	E	G	B	D	F

Space:	1	2	3	4
	F	A	C	E

1. Draw (trace) the Treble Clef on the staff by using the following 4 steps:

Draw a "**J**" from above to below the staff.

Start at the top of the "**J**" and draw a "**P**" to line 4.

Draw a "**d**" from line 4 all the way down to line 1.

Circle up to line 3 and curl, end on line 2 "**G**".

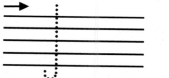 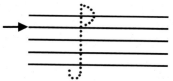 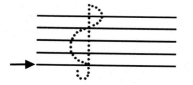 

2. Draw a Treble Clef at the beginning of the staff. Draw a whole note on each given line and space.
Draw a line connecting the Treble Clef notes to the keyboard (at the correct pitch). Name the notes.

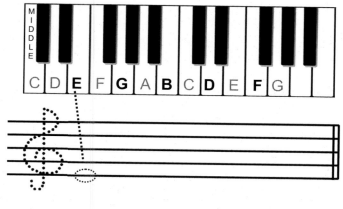 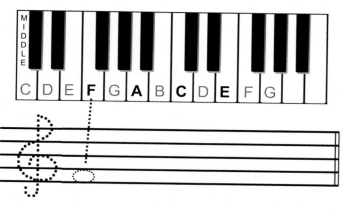

Line:	1	2	3	4	5
	E	___	___	___	___

Space:	1	2	3	4
	F	___	___	___

BASS CLEF - 5 LINES (G, B, D, F, A) and 4 SPACES (A, C, E, G)

Music written in the Treble Clef is usually played with the Right Hand (RH). Music written in the Bass Clef is usually played with the Left Hand (LH).

The **BASS CLEF** or **F CLEF** is drawn on the STAFF. Music notes written in the Bass Clef (or Bass Staff) are drawn as a circle (oval shape) called a Whole Note.

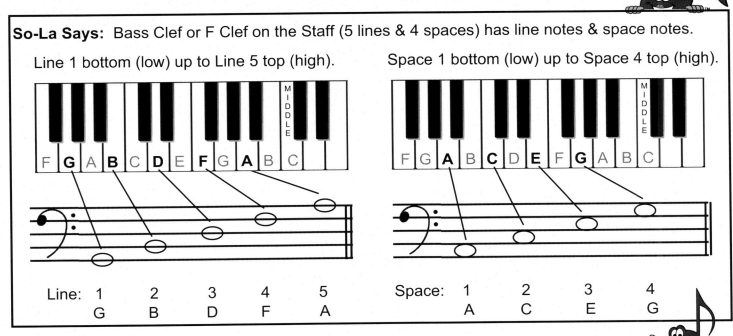

So-La Says: Bass Clef or F Clef on the Staff (5 lines & 4 spaces) has line notes & space notes.

Line 1 bottom (low) up to Line 5 top (high).

Space 1 bottom (low) up to Space 4 top (high).

Line:	1	2	3	4	5
	G	B	D	F	A

Space:	1	2	3	4
	A	C	E	G

1. Draw (trace) the Bass Clef on the staff by using the following 4 steps:

Draw a DOT on line 4. This is the "F" line.

Draw **half of a heart** up to line 5, down to space 1.

Draw a DOT in space 4 (above the "F" line).

Draw a DOT in space 3 (below the "F" line).

2. Draw a Bass Clef at the beginning of the staff. Draw a whole note on each given line and space.
Draw a line connecting the Bass Clef notes to the keyboard (at the correct pitch). Name the notes.

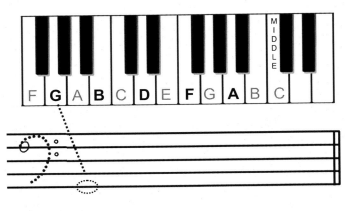

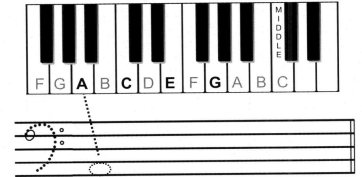

Line:	1	2	3	4	5
	G	___	___	___	___

Space:	1	2	3	4
	A	___	___	___

STAFF - COUNTING INTERVALS - FIRST (SAME) and SECOND (STEP)

An **Interval** is the distance from one note on the staff to the next note on the staff.
An **Interval Number** can be 1, 2, 3, 4, 5, 6, 7 or 8.

To count an Interval Number, always start by counting the **lower note** as **1**. The lower note may be the first or the second note in the Interval.

When the Pattern Direction is going **UP**, the lower note in the Interval will be the first note.
When the Pattern Direction is going **DOWN**, the lower note in the Interval will be the second note.

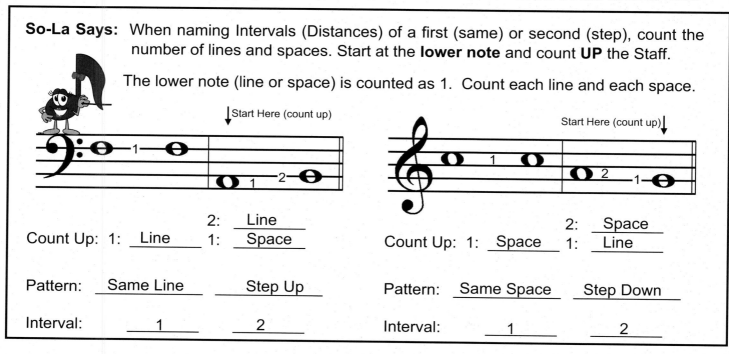

So-La Says: When naming Intervals (Distances) of a first (same) or second (step), count the number of lines and spaces. Start at the **lower note** and count **UP** the Staff.

The lower note (line or space) is counted as 1. Count each line and each space.

Start Here (count up)

Count Up: 1: Line   2: Line / 1: Space

Pattern: Same Line   Step Up

Interval: 1   2

Start Here (count up)

Count Up: 1: Space   2: Space / 1: Line

Pattern: Same Space   Step Down

Interval: 1   2

♫ **Ti-Do Tip:** A **first** (same) is written from a Line Note to the same Line Note: 1-Line, Same Line or from a Space Note to the same Space Note: 1-Space, Same Space.

A **second** (step) is written from a Line to a Space Note: 1-Line, 2-Space or from a Space Note to a Line Note: 1-Space, 2-Line.

1. Name each Interval (Distance) by following these steps:
   a) Count Up by naming the Spaces and Lines from the Lower Note to the Higher Note.
   b) Name the Pattern and Direction as same line, same space, step up or step down.
   c) Name the Interval Number (1 or 2).

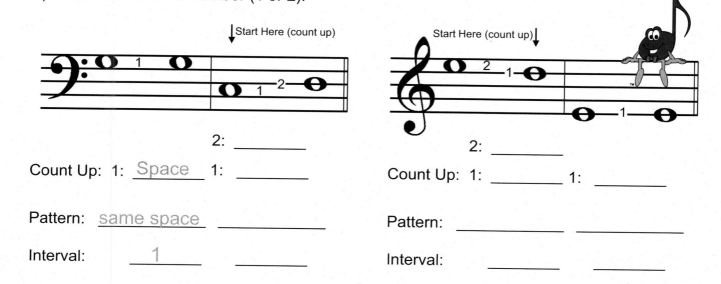

Count Up: 1: Space   2: _____ / 1: _____

Pattern: same space   _____

Interval: 1   _____

Count Up: 1: _____   2: _____ / 1: _____

Pattern: _____   _____

Interval: _____   _____

STAFF - COUNTING INTERVALS - THIRD (SKIP) and FIFTH (LEAP)

So-La Says: When naming Intervals (Distances) of a third (skip) or fifth (leap), count the number of lines and spaces. Start at the **lower note** and count **UP** the Staff.

The lower note (line or space) is counted as 1. Count each line and each space.

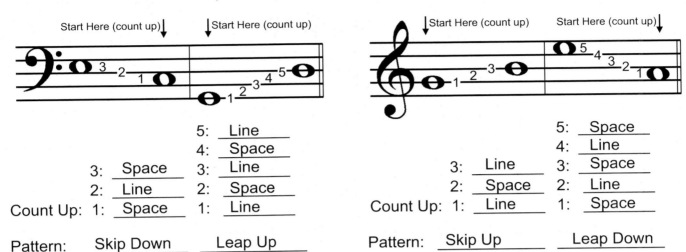

	5:	Line		5:	Space
	4:	Space		4:	Line
3: Space	3:	Line	3: Line	3:	Space
2: Line	2:	Space	2: Space	2:	Line
Count Up: 1: Space	1:	Line	Count Up: 1: Line	1:	Space

Pattern: Skip Down   Leap Up   Pattern: Skip Up   Leap Down

Interval: 3   5   Interval: 3   5

♫ **Ti-Do Tip:** A **third** (skip) is written from a Line Note to a Line Note: 1-Line (2-Space) 3-Line or from a Space Note to a Space Note: 1-Space (2-Line) 3-Space.

A **fifth** (leap) is written from a Line to a Line: 1-Line (2-Space, 3-Line, 4-Space) 5-Line or from a Space Note to a Space Note: 1-Space (2-Line, 3-Space, 4-Line) 5-Space.

1. Name each Interval (Distance) by following these steps:
    a) Count Up by naming the Spaces and Lines from the Lower Note to the Higher Note.
    b) Name the Pattern and Direction as skip up, skip down, leap up or leap down.
    c) Name the Interval Number (3 or 5).

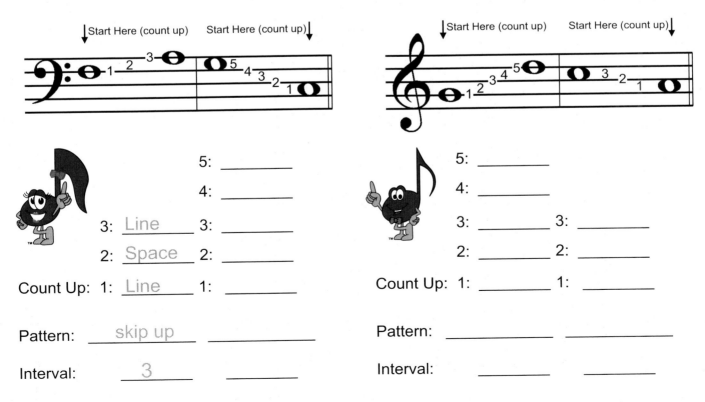

	5: _____		5: _____	
	4: _____		4: _____	
3: Line	3: _____	3: _____	3: _____	
2: Space	2: _____	2: _____	2: _____	
Count Up: 1: Line	1: _____	Count Up: 1: _____	1: _____	

Pattern: _____ skip up _____ _____   Pattern: _____ _____

Interval: _____ 3 _____ _____   Interval: _____ _____

STAFF - COUNTING INTERVALS - EIGHTH (OCTAVE)

So-La Says: When naming Intervals (Distances) of an eighth (octave), count the number of lines and spaces. Start at the **lower note** and count **UP** the Staff.

The lower note (line or space) is counted as 1. Count each line and each space.

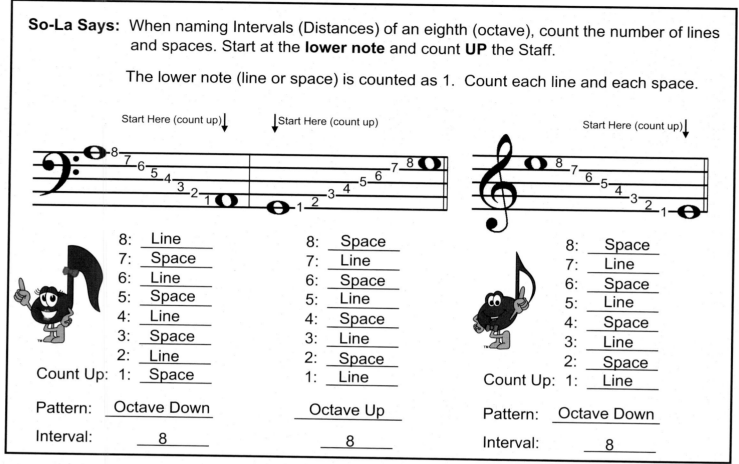

8:	Line
7:	Space
6:	Line
5:	Space
4:	Line
3:	Space
2:	Line
Count Up: 1:	Space

Pattern: Octave Down

Interval: 8

8:	Space
7:	Line
6:	Space
5:	Line
4:	Space
3:	Line
2:	Space
1:	Line

Octave Up

8

8:	Space
7:	Line
6:	Space
5:	Line
4:	Space
3:	Line
2:	Space
Count Up: 1:	Line

Pattern: Octave Down

Interval: 8

♫ **Ti-Do Tip:** An **eighth** (Octave) is written from a Line Note to a Space Note:
1-Line (2-Space, 3-Line, 4-Space, 5-Line, 6-Space, 7-Line) 8-Space
or from a Space Note to a Line Note:
1-Space (2-Line, 3-Space, 4-Line, 5-Space, 6-Line, 7-Space) 8-Line.

1. Write the number of each Line and Space directly in each box on the Staff. Name each Interval.

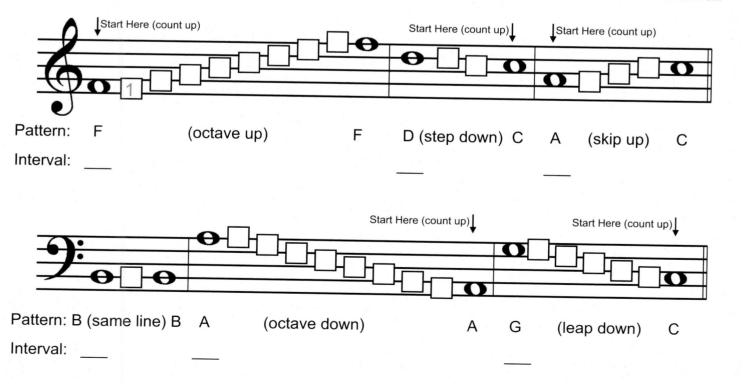

Pattern: F   (octave up)   F   D (step down) C   A   (skip up)   C

Interval: ___   ___   ___

Pattern: B (same line) B   A   (octave down)   A   G   (leap down)   C

Interval: ___   ___   ___

BASS STAFF and TREBLE STAFF - WRITING INTERVALS

The **Distance of a first** (same, 1) is written from:
 a line to the same line (count: same line = 1)
 or a space to the same space (count: same space = 1).

The **Distance of a second** (step, 2) is written from:
 a line to the next space (count: line, space = 2)
 or a space to the next line (count: space, line = 2).

The **Distance of a third** (skip, 3) is written from:
 a line to the next line (count: line, space, line = 3)
 or a space to the next space (count: space, line, space = 3).

The **Distance of a fifth** (leap, 5) is written from:
 a line to a line (count: line, space, line, space, line = 5)
 or a space to a space (count: space, line, space, line, space = 5).

The **Distance of an eighth** (octave, 8) is written from:
 a line to a space
    (count: line, space, line, space, line, space, line, space = 8)
 or a space to a line
    (count: space, line, space, line, space, line, space, line = 8).

♫ **Ti-Do Tip:** When drawn by hand, a whole note is a circle (oval).

1. Write the notes in the Bass Clef and Treble Clef for each Pattern. Use whole notes.
   Name the Interval Number.

Pattern: B (leap up) F   A (octave down) A   F (octave up) F   D (skip down) B

Interval: ___   ___   ___   ___

Pattern: G (skip down) E   C (same space) C   F (step up) G   B (leap down) E

Interval: ___   ___   ___   ___

Lesson 2 Review with So-La & Ti-Do

Check:

1. For the Distance below each bracket:
   WRITE the Numbers to count each note/key (1, 2, 3, etc.) directly on the keyboard.
   WRITE the Note Name of each note/key (A, B, C, etc.).
   WRITE the Pattern (same - line or space, step, skip, leap or octave - up or down).
   WRITE the Interval Number (1, 2, 3, 5 or 8).

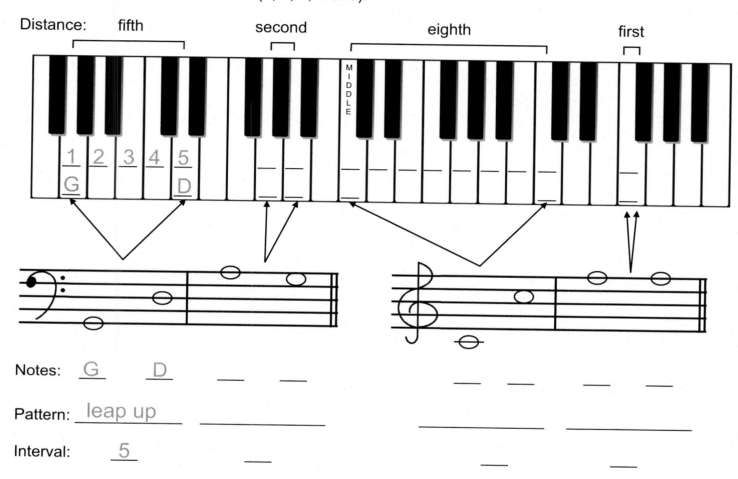

Notes: G   D   ___   ___

Pattern: leap up _____   _____   _____

Interval: 5   ___   ___   ___

2. NAME the notes for each Pattern. Observe the Direction (up or down) for each Pattern.
   WRITE the notes in the Bass Clef and Treble Clef. Use whole notes.
   NAME the Interval Number. PLAY each interval on the piano.

Notes: ___ ___   ___ ___   ___ ___   ___ ___

Pattern: skip down   octave up   leap up   step down

Interval: ___   ___   ___   ___

Lesson 2 Review Ultimate Sight Reading & Ear Training Games

1. COMPLETE each Interval Pattern by adding the word line or the word space.
   TRACE each whole note. NAME the notes.
   PLAY each interval on the piano.

Interval: 1

The distance of a first (same) is written from:

a line note to the same ___line___ note or

a space note to the same _____ note.

F __ __ __ __

Interval: 2

The distance of a second (step) is written from:

a line note to the next _____ note or

a space note to the next _____ note.

__ __ __ __

Interval: 3

The distance of a third (skip) is written from:

a line note to a _____ note or

a space note to a _____ note.

__ __ __ __

Interval: 5

The distance of a fifth (leap) is written from:

a line note to a _____ note or

a space note to a _____ note.

__ __ __ __

Interval: 8

The distance of an eighth (octave) is written from:

a line note to a _____ note or

a space note to a _____ note.

__ __ __ __

Lesson 3 Treble Clef - Landmark Notes and Middle C to High G

Treble Clef Landmark Notes: Middle C, Treble G, Treble C, High G

Landmark Note Middle C is written below the Treble Staff on a ledger line.
Landmark Note Treble G is written on the "G" line, line 2.

Landmark Note Treble C is written in space 3. Space number 3 - That's Treble C.
Landmark Note HIGH G is written in the space ABOVE the Treble Staff.

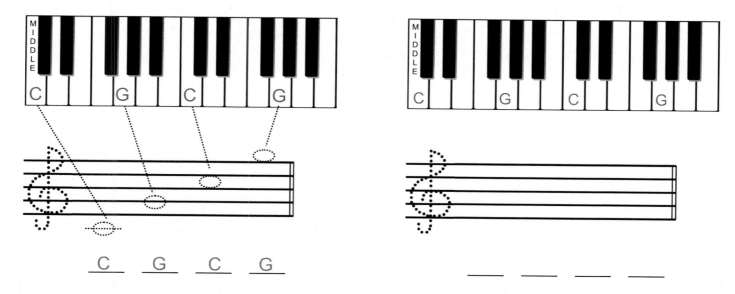

1. Fill in the blanks.

   a) Landmark Note Middle C is written below the Treble Staff on a _____ line.

   b) Landmark Note Treble G is written on the "G" line, line number _____.

   c) Landmark Note Treble C is written in a space, space number _____ - That's Treble C.

   d) Landmark Note High G is written in the space _____ the Treble Staff.

♫ **Ti-Do Tip:** Always use a ruler to draw a straight ledger line below the Treble Staff for Middle C.

2. On each staff, draw a Treble Clef. Write the Landmark Notes Middle C, Treble G, Treble C, High G.
    Use whole notes. Draw a line connecting the notes to the keyboard. Name the notes.

TREBLE CLEF - PATTERNS FROM LANDMARK NOTES

On the Treble Staff, movement between Landmark Notes Middle C, Treble G, Treble C and High G may move by step (2), skip (3), leap (5) or octave (8). A Landmark Note may also be repeated (same).

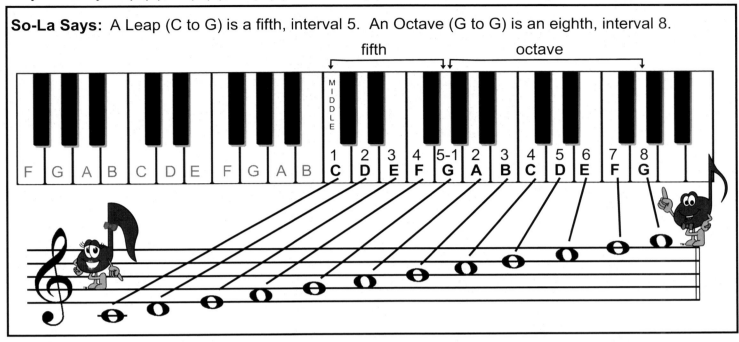

So-La Says: A Leap (C to G) is a fifth, interval 5. An Octave (G to G) is an eighth, interval 8.

1. A Leap (C to G) is a _____, interval ___. An Octave (G to G) is an _____, interval ___.

2. Following the Pattern, add the missing notes. Use whole notes. Name the missing notes.

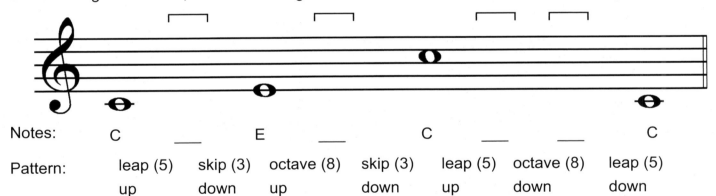

Notes:	C	___	E	___	C	___	___	C

Pattern:	leap (5)	skip (3)	octave (8)	skip (3)	leap (5)	octave (8)	leap (5)
	up	down	up	down	up	down	down

2. Name the notes. Draw a line connecting the notes to the keyboard (at the correct pitch).

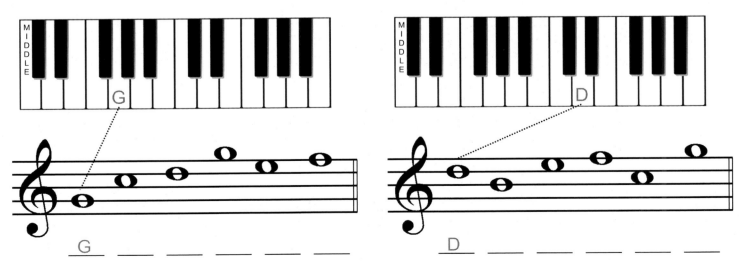

_G_ _ __ __ __ __ __ __   _D_ _ __ __ __ __ __ __

TREBLE CLEF - MIDDLE C UP to HIGH G

Treble Clef notes may move from a MIDDLE sound (pitch) UP to a HIGH sound (pitch). Notes moving from Middle C to High G (space above the Treble Staff) become HIGHER in sound (pitch).

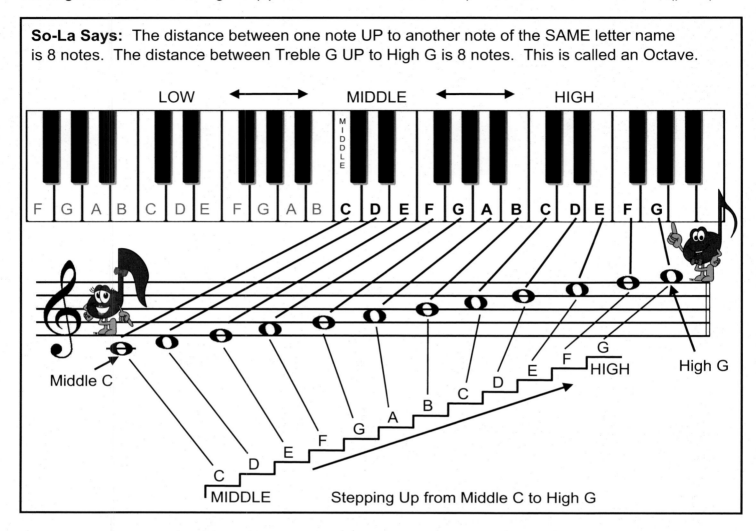

So-La Says: The distance between one note UP to another note of the SAME letter name is 8 notes. The distance between Treble G UP to High G is 8 notes. This is called an Octave.

Stepping Up from Middle C to High G

1. Name the notes - Middle C UP to High G. <u>C</u> <u>D</u> __ __ __ __ __ __ __ __ __ __ __

2. Draw a line connecting the Treble Clef notes to the keyboard (at the correct pitch). Name the notes.

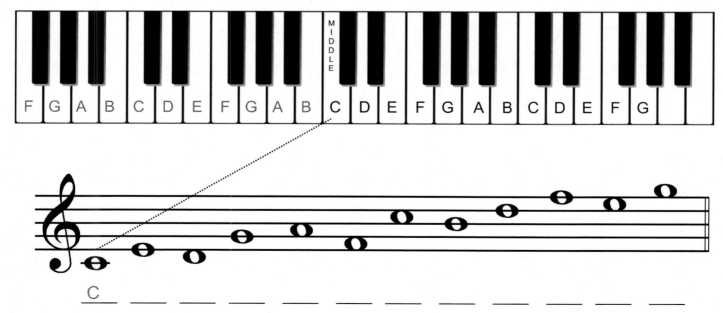

<u>C</u> __ __ __ __ __ __ __ __ __ __ __

TREBLE CLEF - HIGH G DOWN to MIDDLE C

Treble Clef notes may move from a HIGH sound (pitch) DOWN to a MIDDLE sound (pitch). Notes moving from High G to Middle C (ledger line below the Treble Staff) become LOWER in sound (pitch).

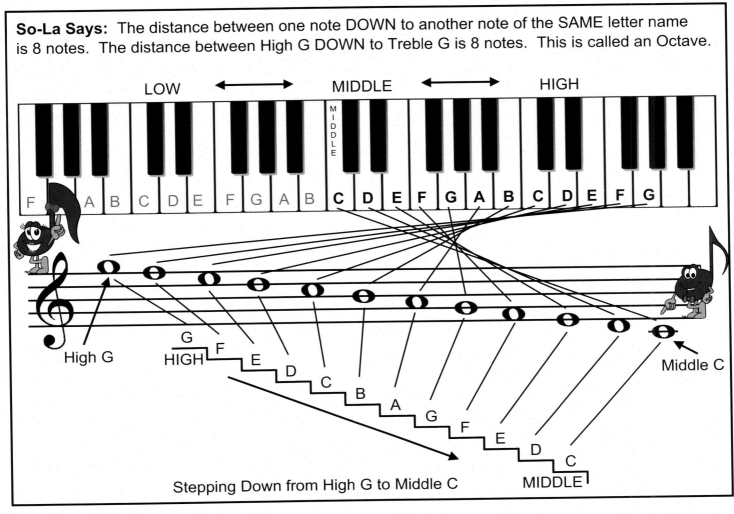

So-La Says: The distance between one note DOWN to another note of the SAME letter name is 8 notes. The distance between High G DOWN to Treble G is 8 notes. This is called an Octave.

Stepping Down from High G to Middle C

1. Name the notes - High G DOWN to Middle C. G F __ __ __ __ __ __ __ __

2. Draw a line connecting the Treble Clef notes to the keyboard (at the correct pitch). Name the notes.

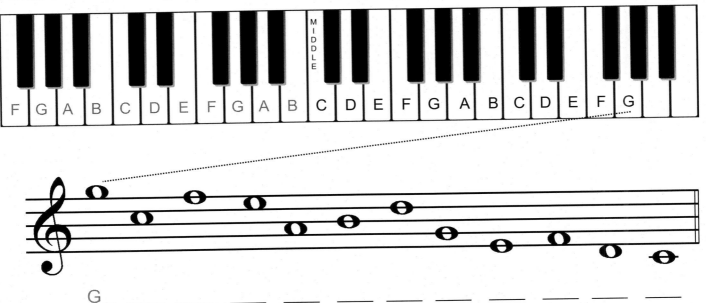

G __ __ __ __ __ __ __ __ __

TREBLE CLEF - MIDDLE C and LINE NOTES E, G, B, D, F

So-La Says: Treble Clef LINE notes are E, G, B, D, F. Line: 1 **E**, 2 **G**, 3 **B**, 4 **D**, 5 **F**.
Landmark Note Middle C is below the Treble Staff on its own ledger line.

As seen in music:

As drawn by hand:

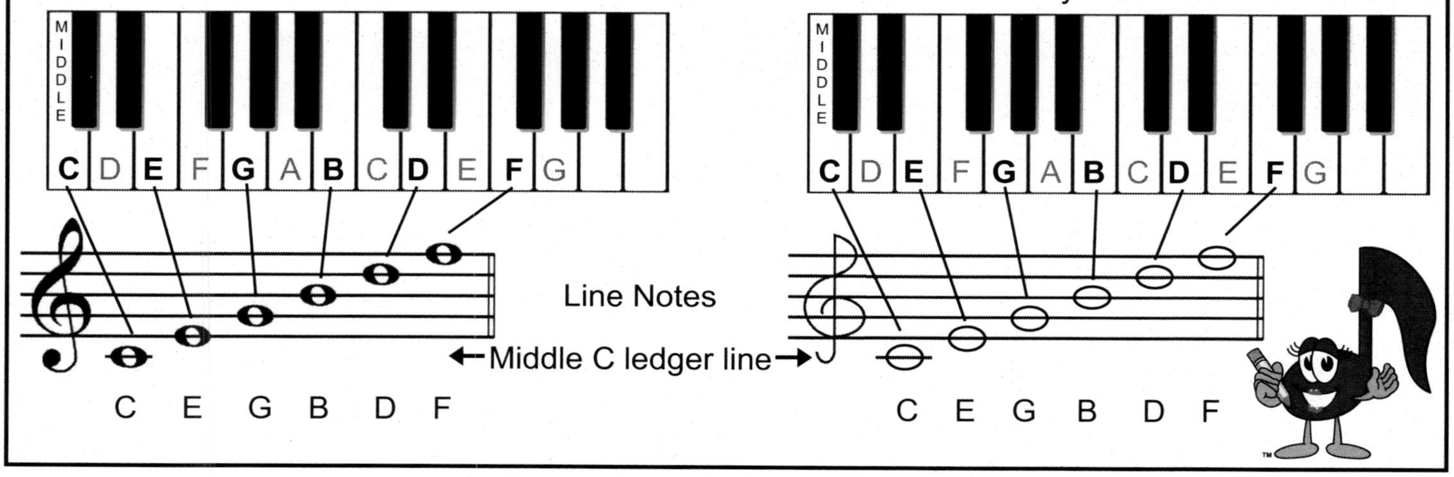

Line Notes

← Middle C ledger line →

C   E   G   B   D   F

C   E   G   B   D   F

1. Name the Treble Clef line notes: Line 1 ___, Line 2 ___, Line 3 ___, Line 4 ___, Line 5 ___.

2. The ledger line note below the Treble Staff is _____ _____.

3. Name the line notes. Draw a line connecting the notes to the keyboard (at the correct pitch).

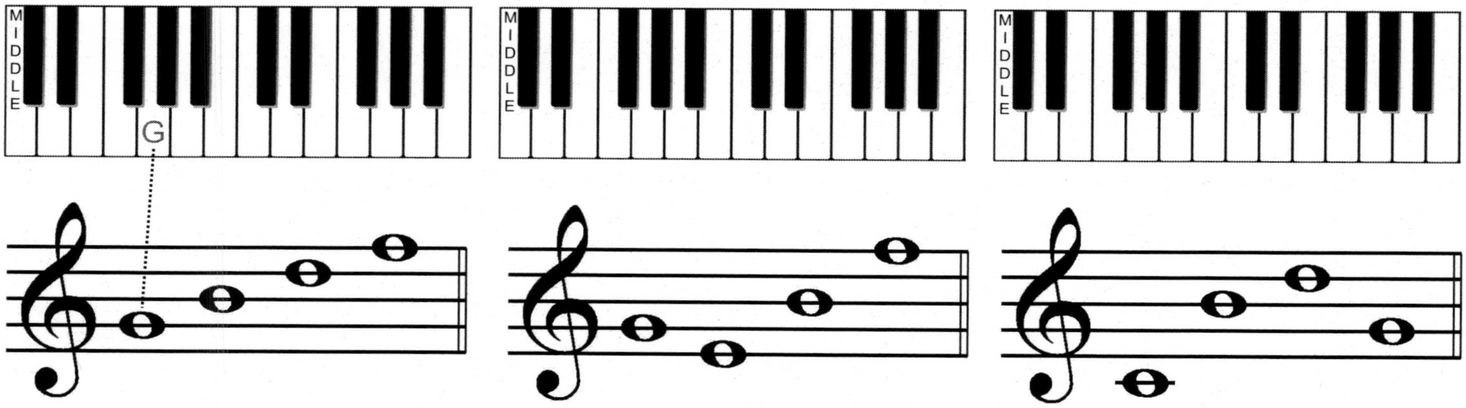

G

___ ___ ___ ___ ___   ___ ___ ___ ___ ___   ___ ___ ___ ___ ___

4. On each staff, draw a Treble Clef. Write the following line notes. Use whole notes.

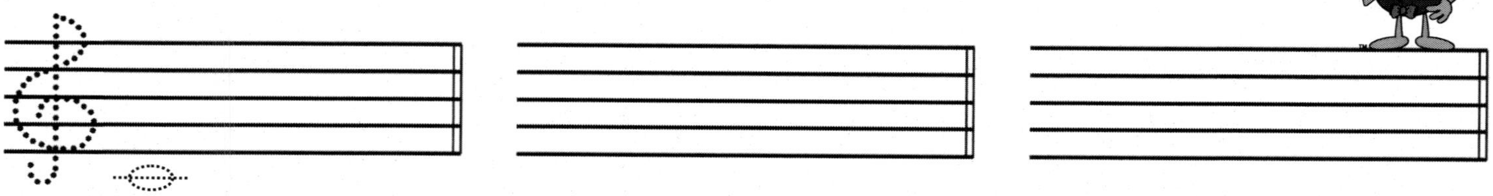

Middle C   D   B   F   E   G   F   D   Middle C   G   E   B

TREBLE CLEF - SPACE NOTES D, G and SPACE NOTES F, A, C, E

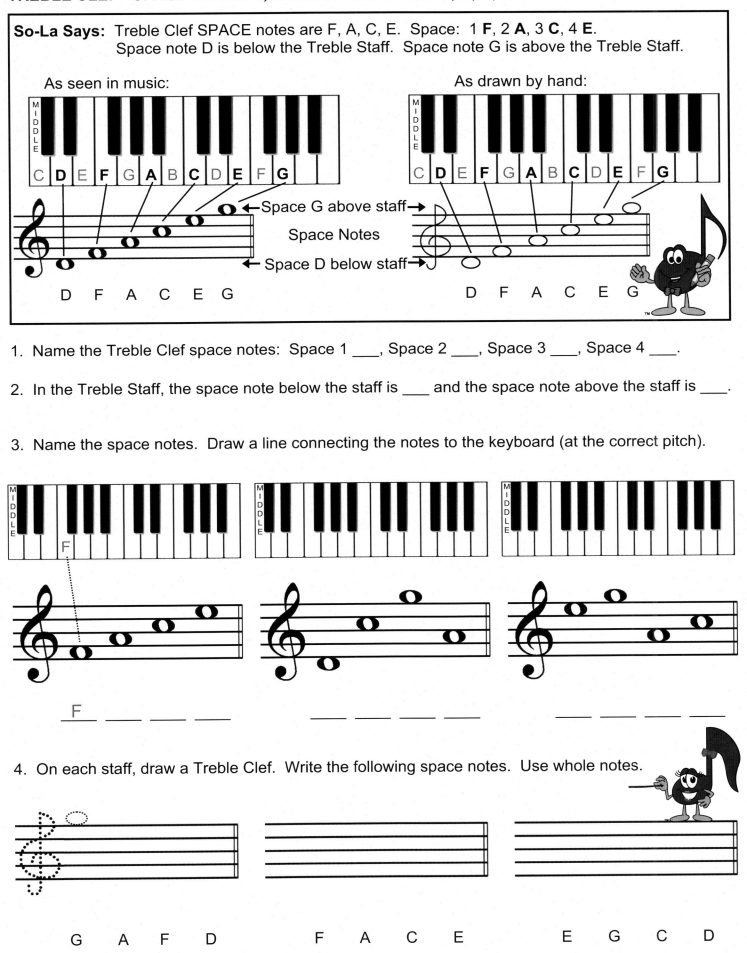

So-La Says: Treble Clef SPACE notes are F, A, C, E. Space: 1 **F**, 2 **A**, 3 **C**, 4 **E**.
Space note D is below the Treble Staff. Space note G is above the Treble Staff.

As seen in music:

As drawn by hand:

Space G above staff →

Space Notes

← Space D below staff →

D F A C E G

D F A C E G

1. Name the Treble Clef space notes: Space 1 ___, Space 2 ___, Space 3 ___, Space 4 ___.

2. In the Treble Staff, the space note below the staff is ___ and the space note above the staff is ___.

3. Name the space notes. Draw a line connecting the notes to the keyboard (at the correct pitch).

F

F ___ ___ ___ ___   ___ ___ ___ ___   ___ ___ ___ ___

4. On each staff, draw a Treble Clef. Write the following space notes. Use whole notes.

G   A   F   D   F   A   C   E   E   G   C   D

Lesson 3 Review with So-La & Ti-Do

Check:

1. On each staff, draw a Treble Clef. Write the Landmark Notes. Use whole notes.

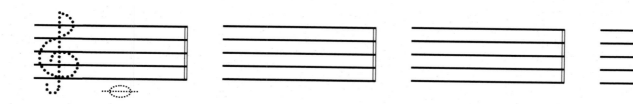

Note: Middle C   Treble G   Treble C   High G

2. Name the notes. Draw a line connecting the notes to the keyboard (at the correct pitch).
    Name the key directly on the keyboard.

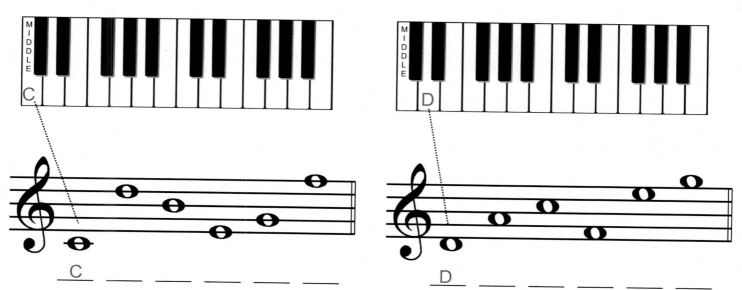

3. Following the Pattern, add the missing notes. Use whole notes. Name the missing notes.

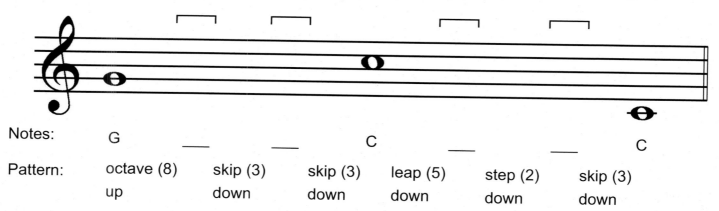

Notes: G   ___   ___   C   ___   ___   C

Pattern: octave (8)   skip (3)   skip (3)   leap (5)   step (2)   skip (3)
            up   down   down   down   down   down

Lesson 3 Review Ultimate Sight Reading & Ear Training Games

1. NAME the notes below the Pattern on each staff.
    WRITE the correct Direction (up or down) for each Pattern.
    PLAY the notes on each staff on the piano.

    LISTEN as your Teacher plays one of the patterns. Is your Teacher playing the
    pattern that is going UP or going DOWN? Color the correct Roller Coaster Car.

a)

Notes: ___ ___ ___ ___ ___ ___ ___ ___   ___ ___ ___ ___ ___ ___ ___ ___

Direction: skipping _____   skipping _____

b)

Notes: ___ ___ ___ ___ ___ ___ ___ ___   ___ ___ ___ ___ ___ ___ ___ ___

Direction: stepping _____   stepping _____

c)

Notes: ___ ___ ___ ___ ___ ___   ___ ___ ___ ___ ___ ___

Direction: skipping _____   skipping _____

Imagine, Compose, Explore!

Imagine So-La and Ti-Do are riding a Roller Coaster!

Compose a song using the white keys on the piano.

Explore the sound as the Roller Coaster goes up HIGH & down LOW.
End on the SAME note as the ride comes to an end.

Lesson 4 Bass Clef - Landmark Notes and Low F to Middle C

Bass Clef Landmark Notes: Low F, Bass C, Bass F, Middle C

Landmark Note Middle C is written above the Bass Staff on a ledger line.
Landmark Note Bass F is written on the "F" line, line 4.

Landmark Note Bass C is written in space 2. Space number 2 - That's Bass C.
Landmark Note LOW F is written in the space BELOW the Bass Staff.

As seen in music: As drawn by hand:

← Middle C →
← Bass F →
← Bass C →
← Low F →

F   C   F   C   F   C   F   C

1. Fill in the blanks.

   a) Landmark Note Middle C is written above the Bass Staff on a _____ line.

   b) Landmark Note Bass F is written on the "F" line, line number _____.

   c) Landmark Note Bass C is written in a space, space number _____ - That's Bass C.

   d) Landmark Note Low F is written in the space _____ the Bass Staff.

♫ **Ti-Do Tip:** Always use a ruler to draw a straight ledger line above the Bass Staff for Middle C.

2. On each staff, draw a Bass Clef. Write the Landmark Notes Low F, Bass C, Bass F and Middle C.
   Use whole notes. Draw a line connecting the notes to the keyboard. Name the notes.

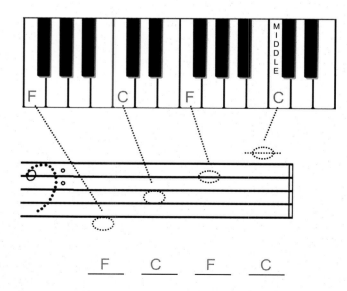

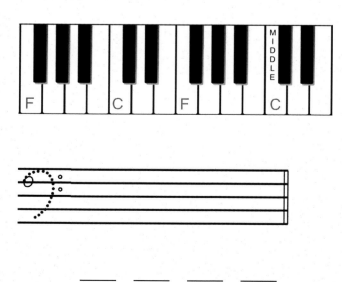

F   C   F   C   ____ ____ ____ ____

BASS CLEF - PATTERNS FROM LANDMARK NOTES

On the Bass Staff, movement between Landmark Notes Low F, Bass C, Bass F and Middle C may move by step (2), skip (3), leap (5) or octave (8). A Landmark Note may also be repeated (same).

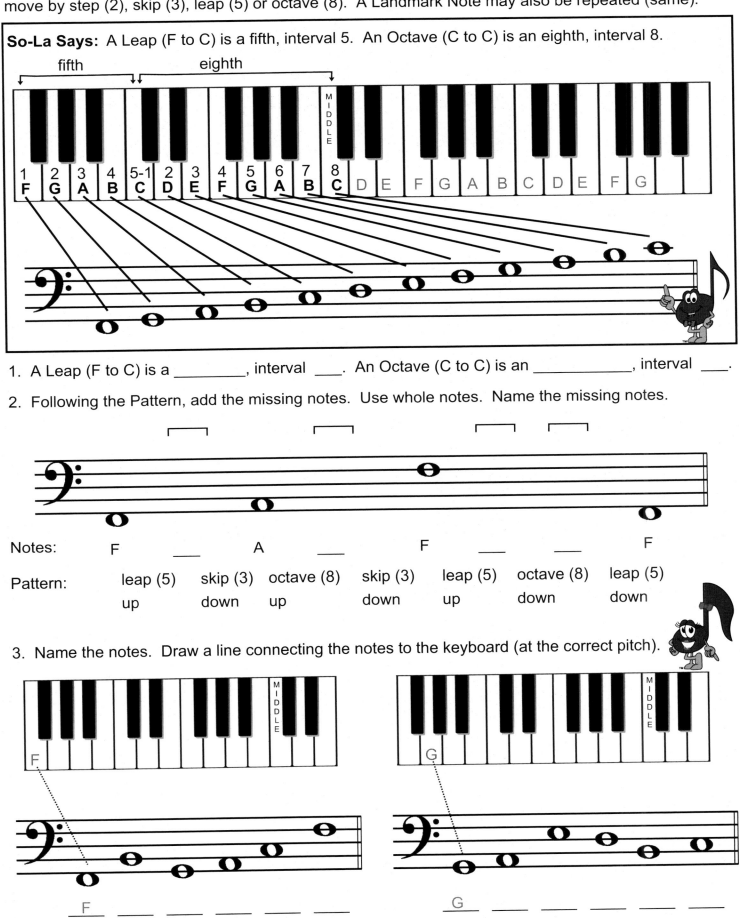

So-La Says: A Leap (F to C) is a fifth, interval 5. An Octave (C to C) is an eighth, interval 8.

1. A Leap (F to C) is a _____, interval ___. An Octave (C to C) is an _____, interval ___.

2. Following the Pattern, add the missing notes. Use whole notes. Name the missing notes.

Notes: F   ___   A   ___   F   ___   ___   F

Pattern: leap (5)   skip (3)   octave (8)   skip (3)   leap (5)   octave (8)   leap (5)
              up   down   up   down   up   down   down

3. Name the notes. Draw a line connecting the notes to the keyboard (at the correct pitch).

F ___ ___ ___ ___ ___

G ___ ___ ___ ___ ___

BASS CLEF - LOW F UP to MIDDLE C

Bass Clef notes may move from a LOW sound (pitch) UP to a MIDDLE sound (pitch). Notes moving from Low F (space below the Bass Staff) to Middle C become HIGHER in sound (pitch).

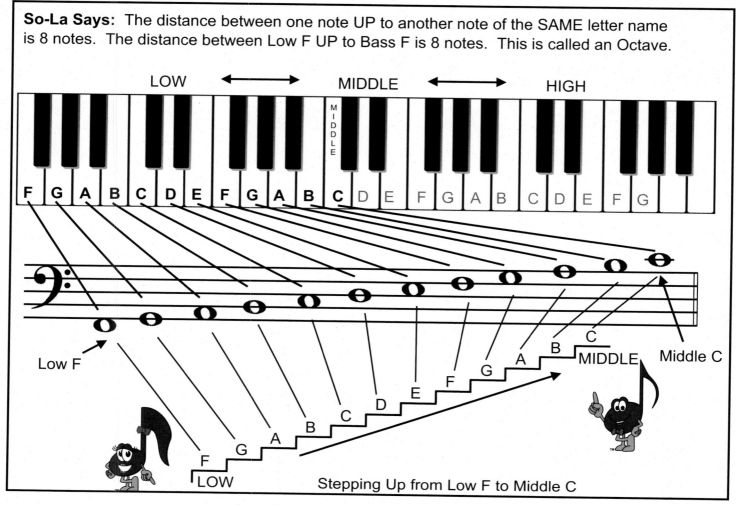

So-La Says: The distance between one note UP to another note of the SAME letter name is 8 notes. The distance between Low F UP to Bass F is 8 notes. This is called an Octave.

Stepping Up from Low F to Middle C

1. Name the notes - Low F UP to Middle C. F G __ __ __ __ __ __ __ __ __ __ __ __ __

2. Draw a line connecting the Bass Clef notes to the keyboard (at the correct pitch). Name the notes.

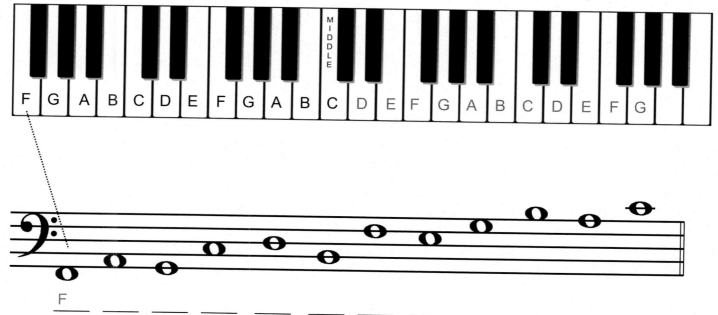

F

BASS CLEF - MIDDLE C DOWN to LOW F

Bass Clef notes may move from a MIDDLE sound (pitch) DOWN to a LOW sound (pitch). Notes moving from Middle C (ledger line above the Bass Staff) to Low F become LOWER in sound (pitch).

So-La Says: The distance between one note DOWN to another note of the SAME letter name is 8 notes. The distance between Bass F DOWN to Low F is 8 notes. This is called an Octave.

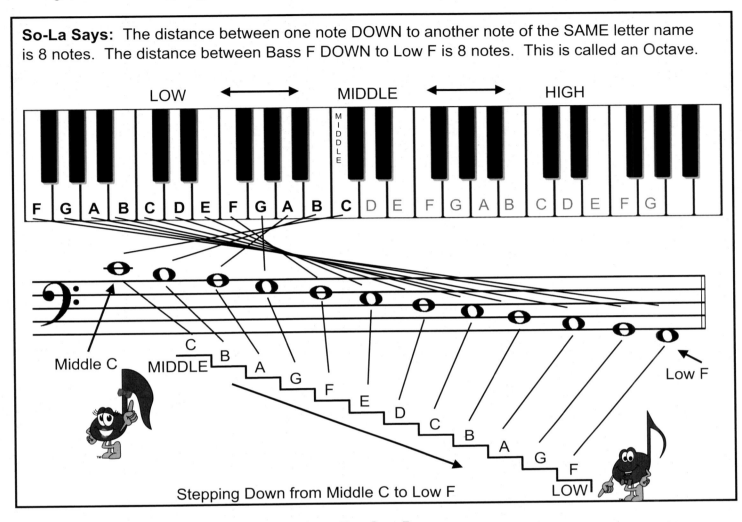

Stepping Down from Middle C to Low F

1. Name the notes - Middle C DOWN to Low F. <u>C</u> <u>B</u> __ __ __ __ __ __ __ __ __ __ __ __

2. Draw a line connecting the Bass Clef notes to the keyboard (at the correct pitch). Name the notes.

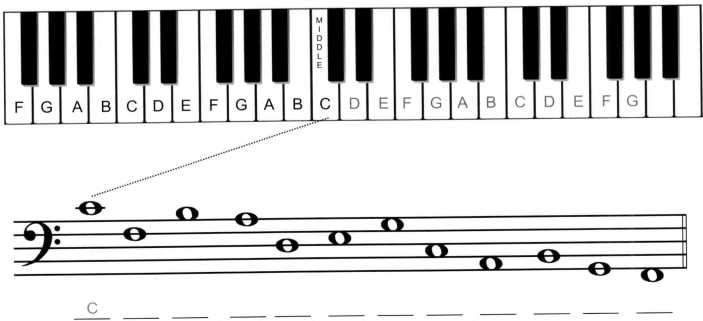

<u>C</u> __ __ __ __ __ __ __ __ __ __ __ __

BASS CLEF - LINE NOTES G, B, D, F, A and MIDDLE C

So-La Says: Bass Clef LINE notes are G, B, D, F, A. Line: 1 **G**, 2 **B**, 3 **D**, 4 **F**, 5 **A**.
Landmark Note Middle C is above the Bass Staff on its own ledger line.

As seen in music:

As drawn by hand:

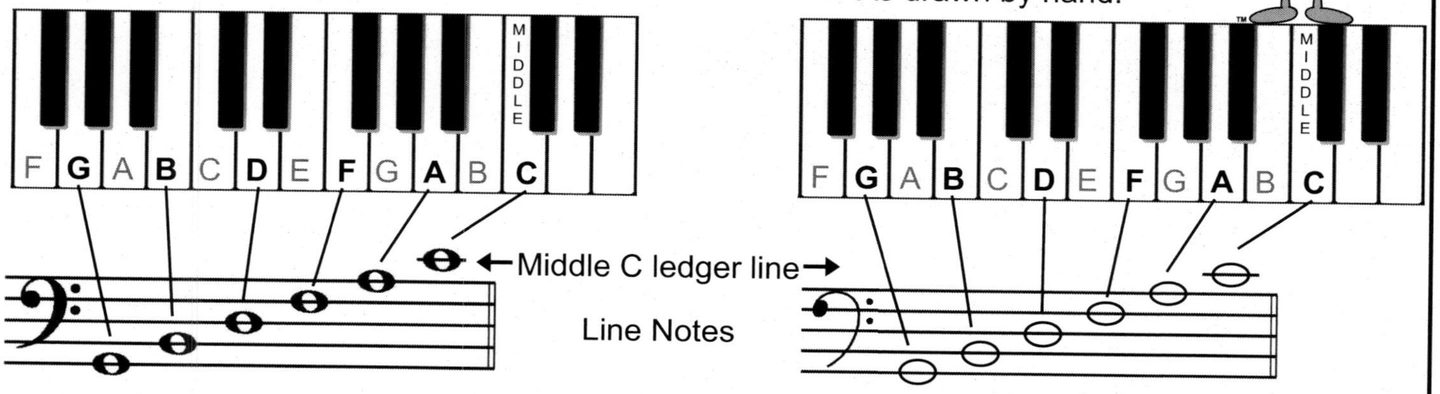

← Middle C ledger line →

Line Notes

G   B   D   F   A   C

G   B   D   F   A   C

1. Name the Bass Clef line notes: Line 1 ___, Line 2 ___, Line 3 ___, Line 4 ___, Line 5 ___.

2. The ledger line note above the Bass Staff is _____ _____.

3. Name the line notes. Draw a line connecting the notes to the keyboard (at the correct pitch).

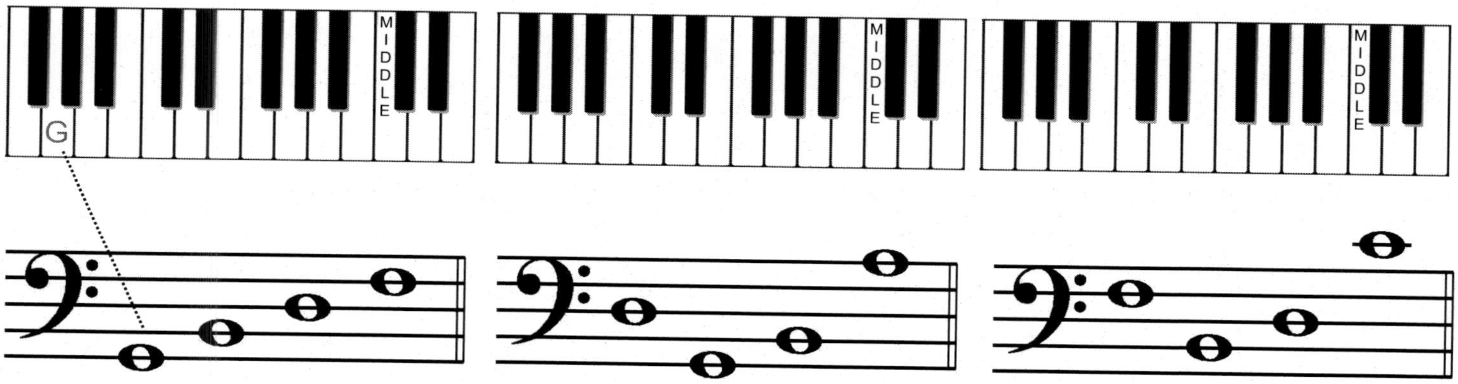

G

___ ___ ___ ___ ___

___ ___ ___ ___

___ ___ ___ ___

4. On each staff, draw a Bass Clef. Write the following line notes. Use whole notes.

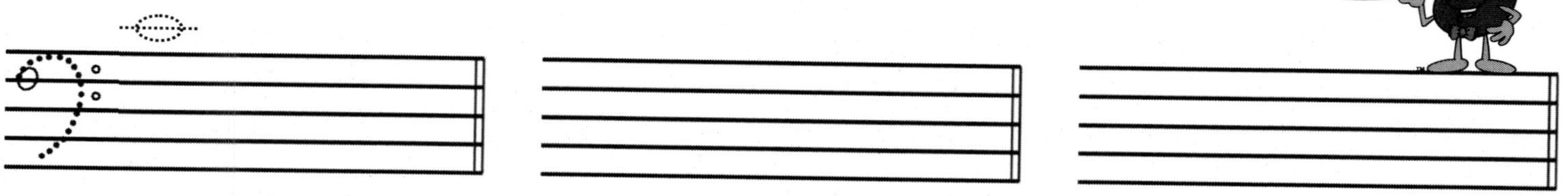

Middle C   A   D   B   G   A   B   F   Middle C   F   G   D

BASS CLEF - SPACE NOTES F, B and SPACE NOTES A, C, E, G

So-La Says: Bass Clef SPACE notes are A, C, E, G. Space: 1 **A**, 2 **C**, 3 **E**, 4 **G**.
Space note F is below the Bass Staff. Space note B is above the Bass Staff.

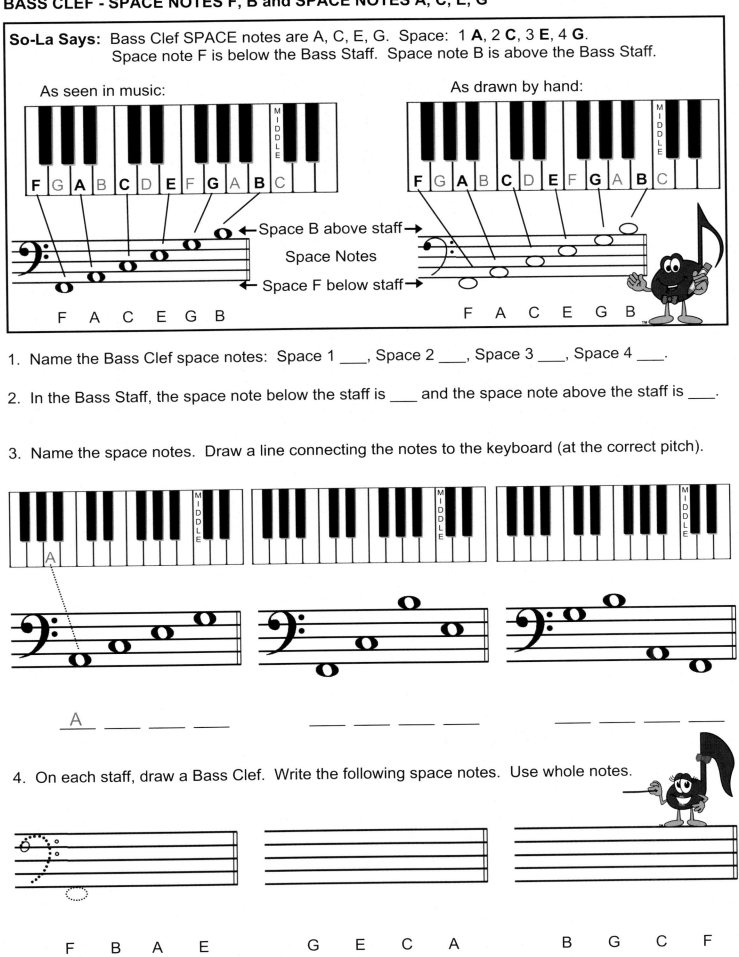

1. Name the Bass Clef space notes: Space 1 ___, Space 2 ___, Space 3 ___, Space 4 ___.

2. In the Bass Staff, the space note below the staff is ___ and the space note above the staff is ___.

3. Name the space notes. Draw a line connecting the notes to the keyboard (at the correct pitch).

A ___ ___ ___ ___   ___ ___ ___ ___   ___ ___ ___ ___

4. On each staff, draw a Bass Clef. Write the following space notes. Use whole notes.

F   B   A   E   G   E   C   A   B   G   C   F

Lesson 4 Review with So-La & Ti-Do

Check:

1. On each staff, draw a Bass Clef. Write the Landmark Notes. Use whole notes.

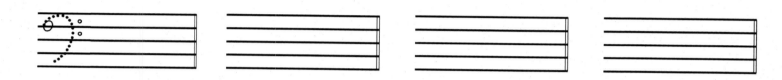

Note: Middle C   Bass F   Bass C   Low F

2. Name the notes. Draw a line connecting the notes to the keyboard (at the correct pitch). Name the key directly on the keyboard.

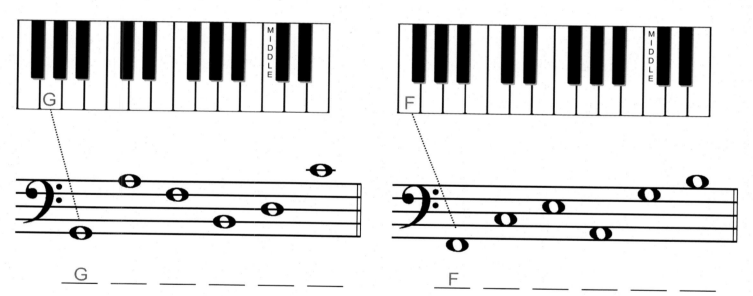

G ___ ___ ___ ___ ___   F ___ ___ ___ ___ ___ ___ ___

3. Following the Pattern, add the missing notes. Use whole notes. Name the missing notes.

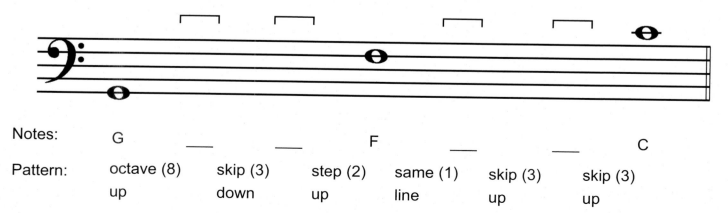

Notes:	G			F			C
Pattern:	octave (8) up	skip (3) down	step (2) up	same (1) line	skip (3) up	skip (3) up	

Lesson 4 Review Ultimate Sight Reading & Ear Training Games

1. WRITE the letter name below each note (A, B, C, D, E, F, G).
    WRITE the Interval Number in each tail (1, 2, 3, 4, 5, 6, 7, 8).

2. PLAY the Intervals in each fish.

Lesson 5 Whole Steps, Half Steps & Pentascale Patterns

WHITE KEYS - WHOLE STEPS and HALF STEPS

Distances between WHITE KEYS on the keyboard are a Whole Step ⌊WS⌋ or a Half Step ⌣HS⌣.
A Whole Step (also called a Whole Tone) is two Half Steps (also called a Semitone).

So-La Says: Whole Step is labelled as ⌊WS⌋ (square bracket). Half Step is labelled as ⌣HS⌣ (slur).

Whole Step ⌊WS⌋ is the distance from one white key
to the next white key with ONE black key in between.

Half Step ⌣HS⌣ is the distance from one white key
to the next white key with NO key in between.

The only Half Steps between
white keys are E to F and B to C.   White Key Pattern: WS WS HS WS WS WS HS

C D E F G A B C

---

1. Distance between white keys on the keyboard is a _____ Step (WS) or a _____ Step (HS).

2. The only Half Steps between white keys are _____ to _____ and _____ to _____.

3. Name the distance from one white key to the next as: WS for Whole Step or HS for Half Step.

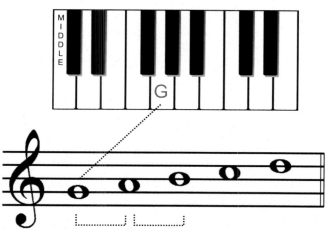

C D   F G   B C   E F   A B   D E   G A

White Key Pattern: ____   ____   ____   ____   ____   ____   ____

4. Draw a line connecting the notes to the keyboard (at the correct pitch). Below the staff, draw a
   square bracket ⌊__⌋ for a Whole Step and a slur ⌣ for a Half Step.

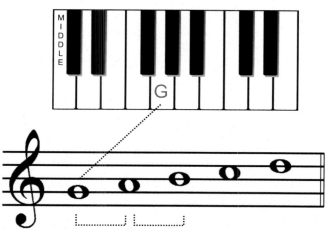

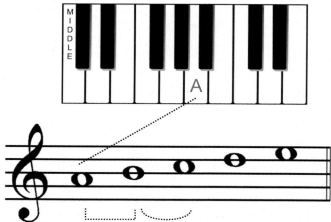

WHOLE STEPS and HALF STEPS - UP or DOWN

A Whole Step or a Half Step may step up or step down. Two Half Steps equals one Whole Step.

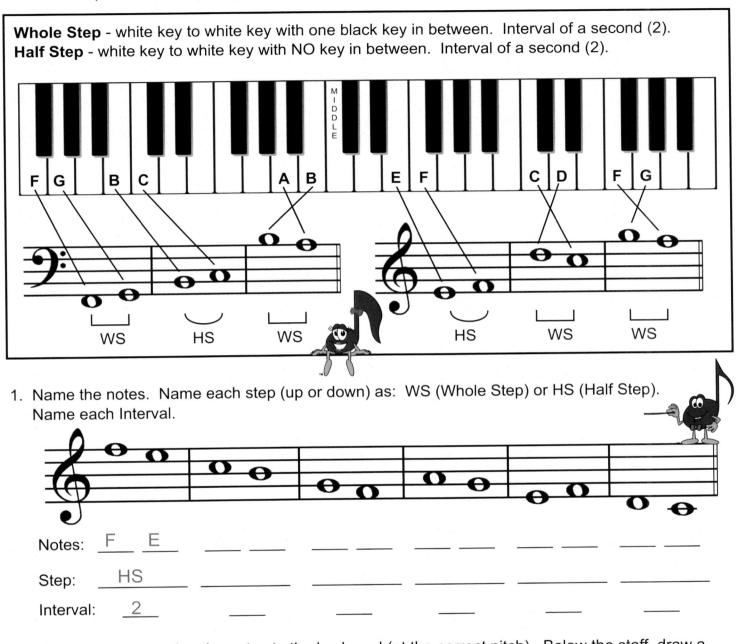

Whole Step - white key to white key with one black key in between. Interval of a second (2).
Half Step - white key to white key with NO key in between. Interval of a second (2).

1. Name the notes. Name each step (up or down) as: WS (Whole Step) or HS (Half Step).
    Name each Interval.

Notes: F E ___ ___ ___ ___ ___ ___ ___ ___ ___ ___

Step: HS ___ ___ ___ ___ ___

Interval: 2 ___ ___ ___ ___ ___

2. Draw a line connecting the notes to the keyboard (at the correct pitch). Below the staff, draw a
    square bracket └──┘ for a Whole Step and a slur ‿ for a Half Step.

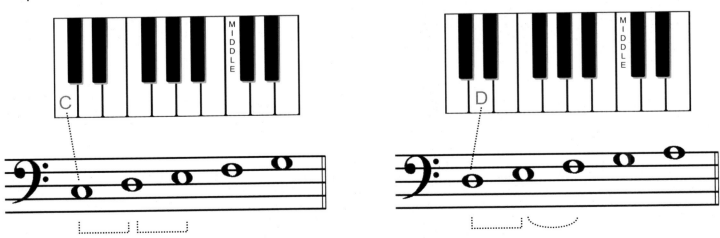

PENTASCALE PATTERN - MAJOR (HAPPY) SOUND ☺

A PENTASCALE (penta means 5) is a pattern of 5 notes moving by step in the same direction.
A MAJOR Pentascale Pattern is 1 - Whole Step - 2 - Whole Step - 3 - Half Step - 4 - Whole Step - 5.

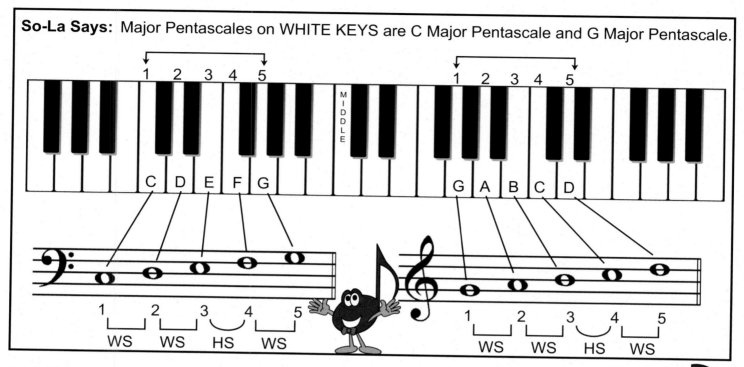

So-La Says: Major Pentascales on WHITE KEYS are C Major Pentascale and G Major Pentascale.

1. A Major Pentascale Pattern has a Major _____ sound.

2. A Major Pentascale is a _____ note pattern moving by step in the same direction.

3. Write the Major Pentascale Pattern of Whole Steps and Half Step:

    1 - _____ step - 2 - _____ step - 3 - _____ step - 4 - _____ step - 5

4. Major Pentascales on white keys are _____ Major Pentascale and _____ Major Pentascale.

5. Draw a line connecting the notes to the keyboard (at the correct pitch). Below the staff, draw a square bracket └──┘ for a Whole Step and a slur ◡ for a Half Step.

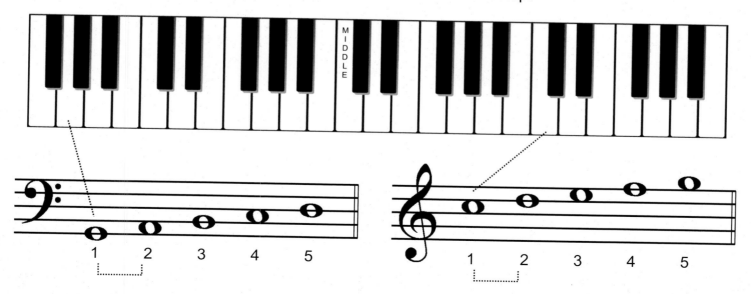

PENTASCALE PATTERN - MINOR (SAD) SOUND 🙁

A PENTASCALE (penta means 5) is a pattern of 5 notes moving by step in the same direction.
A MINOR Pentascale Pattern is: 1 - Whole Step - 2 - Half Step - 3 - Whole Step - 4 - Whole Step - 5.

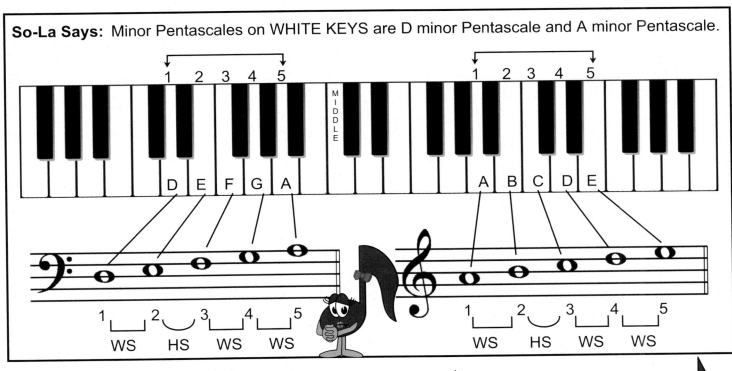

1. A minor Pentascale Pattern has a minor _____ sound.

2. A minor Pentascale is a _____ note pattern moving by step in the same direction.

3. Write the minor Pentascale Pattern of Whole Steps and Half Step:

   1 - _____ step - 2 - _____ step - 3 - _____ step - 4 - _____ step - 5

4. Minor Pentascales on white keys are _____ minor Pentascale and _____ minor Pentascale.

5. Draw a line connecting the notes to the keyboard (at the correct pitch). Below the staff, draw a square bracket ⌐_⌐ for a Whole Step and a slur ⌣ for a Half Step.

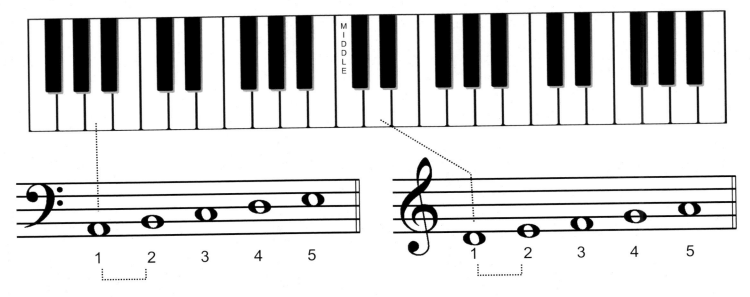

Lesson 5 Review with So-La & Ti-Do

Check:

1. Name the notes. Name each step (up or down) as: WS (Whole Step) or HS (Half Step). Draw a line connecting the notes to the keyboard (at the correct pitch).

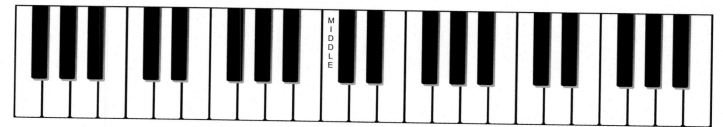

Notes: ____ ____ ____ ____ ____ ____ ____ ____ ____ ____

Step: _____ _____ _____   _____ _____ _____

2. Add the Whole Steps and Half Step to complete each Pentascale Pattern:

Major: 1 - _____ step - 2 - _____ step - 3 - _____ step - 4 - _____ step - 5

minor: 1 - _____ step - 2 - _____ step - 3 - _____ step - 4 - _____ step - 5

3. Draw a line connecting the notes to the keyboard (at the correct pitch). Below the staff, draw a square bracket ⌊_⌋ for a Whole Step and a slur ‿ for a Half Step. Name each Pentascale as Major or minor.

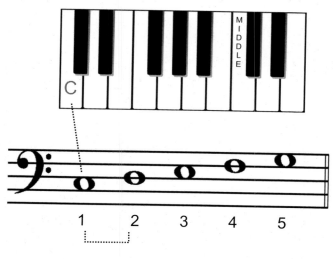
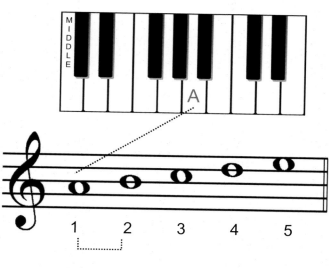

Pentascale: C _____ Pentascale   A _____ Pentascale

Lesson 5 Review Ultimate Sight Reading & Ear Training Games

1.   Below each Pentascale:
DRAW a square bracket ⌊__⌋ for a Whole Step and a slur ⌣ for a Half Step.
NAME the notes.
PLAY the notes on each staff on the piano. NAME each Pentascale as Major or minor.

LISTEN as your Teacher plays one of the patterns. Is your Teacher playing the
MAJOR (happy) Pentascale or the MINOR (sad) Pentascale? Color the correct star.

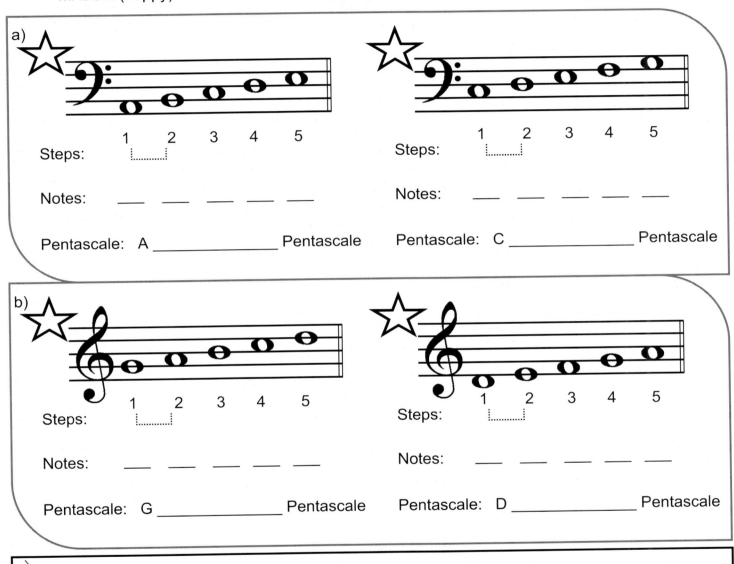

a)

Steps: 1   2   3   4   5

Notes: __   __   __   __   __

Pentascale: A _____ Pentascale

Steps: 1   2   3   4   5

Notes: __   __   __   __   __

Pentascale: C _____ Pentascale

b)

Steps: 1   2   3   4   5

Notes: __   __   __   __   __

Pentascale: G _____ Pentascale

Steps: 1   2   3   4   5

Notes: __   __   __   __   __

Pentascale: D _____ Pentascale

Imagine, **C**ompose, **E**xplore!

Imagine So-La and Ti-Do are marching in a Parade with Spot the Dog,
Max the Turtle and Diva the Cat.

Compose a song using the Major and minor Pentascale Patterns.

Explore the happy sound as the sun shines on the Parade.
Explore the sad sound as the clouds rain on the Parade.

Lesson 6 Black Keys - Half Steps - Sharp, Flat & Natural

HALF STEP (HS) or SEMITONE (ST) is the shortest distance between two keys with no key in between. Half step - white key to next black key or black key to next white key.

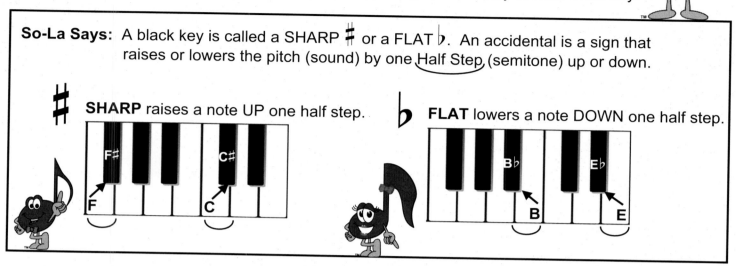

So-La Says: A black key is called a SHARP ♯ or a FLAT ♭. An accidental is a sign that raises or lowers the pitch (sound) by one Half Step (semitone) up or down.

SHARP raises a note UP one half step.

FLAT lowers a note DOWN one half step.

♫ **Ti-Do Tip:** A sharp or flat sign is written in front of a note on the staff and after the letter name.

1. Draw a line connecting the notes to the keyboard (at the correct pitch). Name the notes.

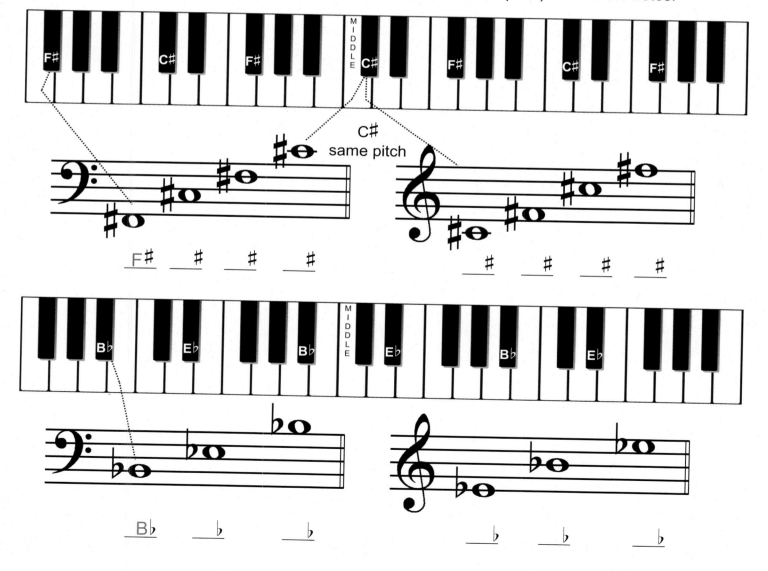

ACCIDENTALS - SHARP, FLAT and NATURAL SIGN

So-La Says: An **ACCIDENTAL** is a sign that raises or lowers the pitch one half step (semitone). A Black Key may be written as a Sharp or a Flat. A Natural is always a White Key.

SHARP

FLAT

NATURAL

A **SHARP RAISES** a note one half step (semitone).

A **FLAT LOWERS** a note one half step (semitone).

A **NATURAL CANCELS** a sharp or a flat (white key).

Sharp sign written as a **number** sign on an **angle**.

Flat sign written as a **line** plus **half of a heart**.

Natural sign written as a letter **L** and number **7**.

$$\# = \sharp$$

$$| + \heartsuit = \flat$$

$$L + 7 = \natural$$

As seen in music:

C♯   D♭   C♮   D♮

As drawn by hand:

C♯   D♭   C♮   D♮

1. Trace the accidentals. Fill in the blanks below.

A Sharp _____ a note one half step (semitone).

A Flat _____ a note one half step (semitone).

A Natural _____ a sharp or a flat (white key).

♫ **Ti-Do Tip:** Accidentals are written in front of a note on the staff and after the letter name.

2. Trace the accidentals in front of each note. Name the notes (with accidental after the letter name).

F♯   _____   _____   _____   _____   _____

_____   _____   _____   _____   _____   _____

BLACK KEYS - SHARPS

So-La Says: A Sharp is written in front of a note and after the letter name. ♯ = UP a half step.

♫ **Ti-Do Tip:** A natural sign cancels a sharp. A natural note is always a white key.

1. Draw a line connecting the notes to the keyboard (at the correct pitch). Name the notes.

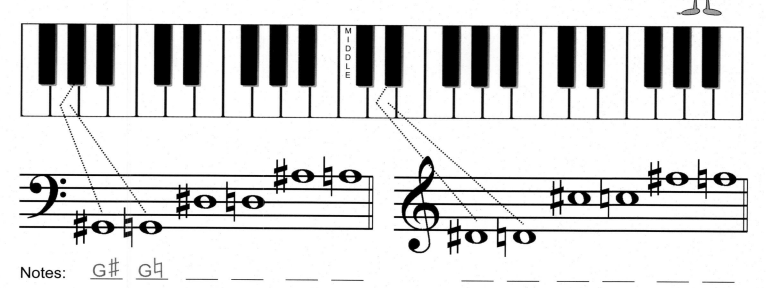

Notes: G♯ G♮ ___ ___ ___ ___ ___ ___

2. Name the notes. Label the Half Steps as HS. Play the notes on the piano and say the note names.

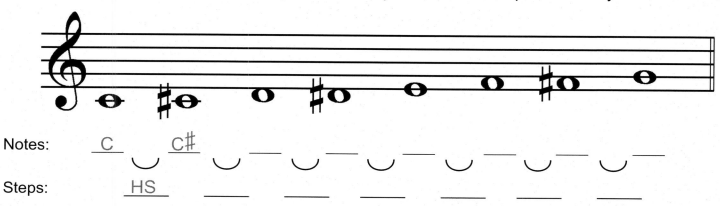

Notes: C   C♯ ___ ___ ___ ___ ___ ___

Steps: HS ___ ___ ___ ___ ___ ___

BLACK KEYS - FLATS

So-La Says: A Flat is written in front of a note and after the letter name. ♭ = DOWN a half step.

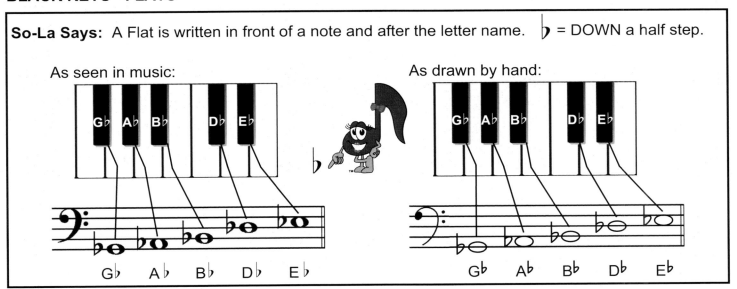

As seen in music:

As drawn by hand:

♫ **Ti-Do Tip:** A natural sign cancels a flat. A natural note is always a white key.

1. Draw a line connecting the notes to the keyboard (at the correct pitch). Name the notes.

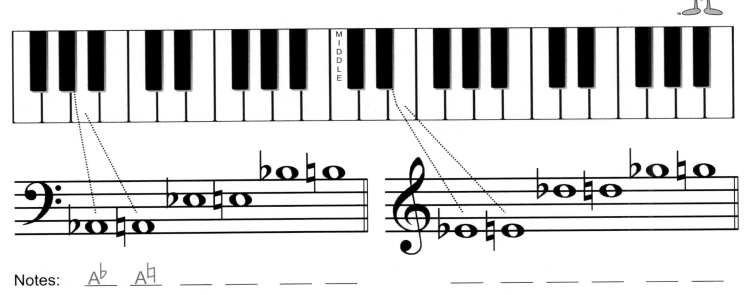

Notes: ___A♭___ ___A♮___ ___ ___ ___ ___ ___ ___

2. Name the notes. Label the Half Steps as HS. Play the notes on the piano and say the note names.

Notes: ___A___ ___B♭___ ___ ___ ___ ___ ___ ___ ___

Steps: ___HS___ ___ ___ ___ ___ ___ ___

Lesson 6 Review with So-La & Ti-Do

Check:

1. Draw a line connecting the notes to the keyboard (at the correct pitch). Name the notes.

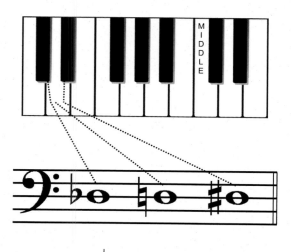

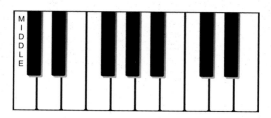

Notes: _____D♭_____ _____ _____

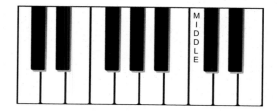

Notes: _____ _____ _____

2. Add the correct accidental (sharp, flat or natural) in front of each whole note on the Treble Staff.

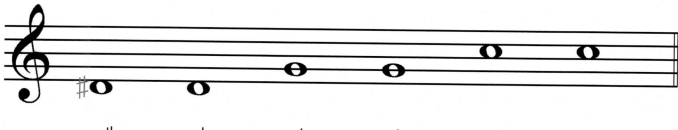

Notes: D♯ D♮ G♭ G♮ C♯ C♮

Lesson 6 Review Ultimate Sight Reading & Ear Training Games

1. NAME the notes.
   PLAY the notes on the piano and say the note names.
   CIRCLE if the Pattern Direction is going Half Steps UP or Half Steps DOWN.

   LISTEN as your Teacher plays one of the Half Steps Patterns. Is your Teacher playing the
   Half Steps UP Pattern or the Half Steps DOWN Pattern? Color the correct pet food bowl.

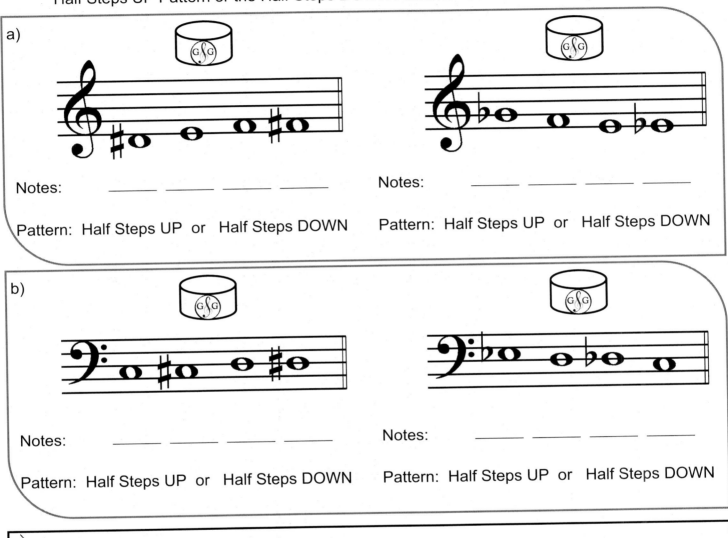

a)

Notes: ___ ___ ___ ___ ___

Pattern: Half Steps UP or Half Steps DOWN

Notes: ___ ___ ___ ___ ___

Pattern: Half Steps UP or Half Steps DOWN

b)

Notes: ___ ___ ___ ___ ___

Pattern: Half Steps UP or Half Steps DOWN

Notes: ___ ___ ___ ___ ___

Pattern: Half Steps UP or Half Steps DOWN

Imagine, Compose, Explore!

Imagine So-La and Ti-Do are going to the Pet Store to buy food for Diva the Cat,
Max the Turtle and Spot the Dog.

Compose a song using the Half Steps UP Patterns and the Half Steps DOWN Patterns.

Explore the Half Steps Up sounds as they walk UP the steps into the store to buy the food.

Explore the Half Steps DOWN sounds as they walk DOWN the steps with the food.

Lesson 7   Pentascale Patterns - G Major/G minor & C Major/C minor

G MAJOR PENTASCALE PATTERN - MAJOR (HAPPY) SOUND ☺

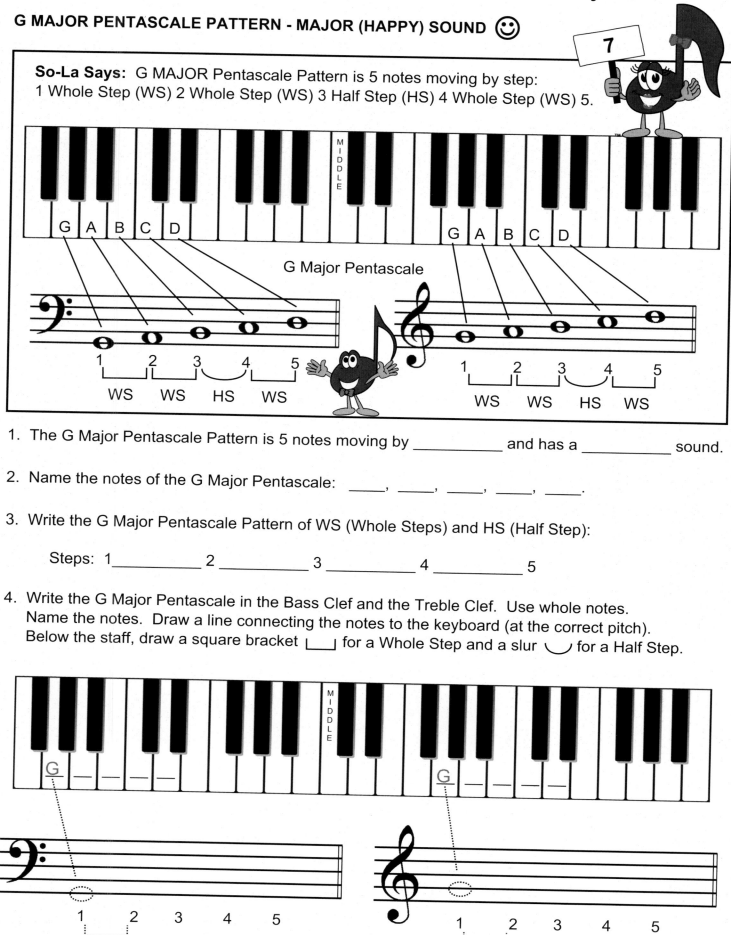

So-La Says: G MAJOR Pentascale Pattern is 5 notes moving by step:
1 Whole Step (WS) 2 Whole Step (WS) 3 Half Step (HS) 4 Whole Step (WS) 5.

1. The G Major Pentascale Pattern is 5 notes moving by _____ and has a _____ sound.

2. Name the notes of the G Major Pentascale: ____, ____, ____, ____, ____.

3. Write the G Major Pentascale Pattern of WS (Whole Steps) and HS (Half Step):

   Steps: 1_____ 2 _____ 3 _____ 4 _____ 5

4. Write the G Major Pentascale in the Bass Clef and the Treble Clef. Use whole notes.
   Name the notes. Draw a line connecting the notes to the keyboard (at the correct pitch).
   Below the staff, draw a square bracket ⌐⌐ for a Whole Step and a slur ⌣ for a Half Step.

G MINOR PENTASCALE PATTERN - MINOR (SAD) SOUND ☹

G MAJOR Pentascale is changed to G MINOR Pentascale by lowering the third note one half step.
The third note B is lowered to B flat. G Major (G, A, B, C, D) to G minor (G, A, B♭, C, D).

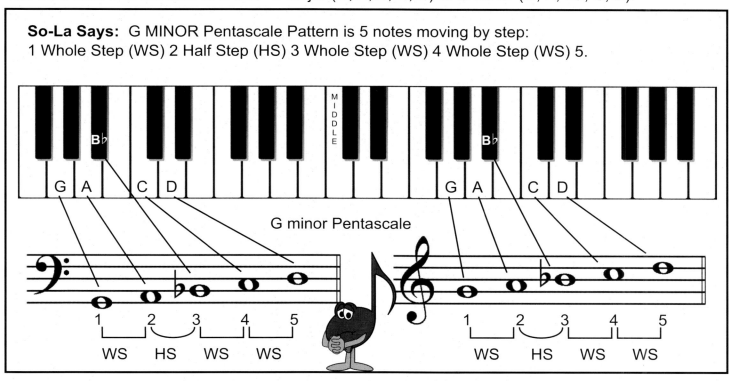

So-La Says: G MINOR Pentascale Pattern is 5 notes moving by step:
1 Whole Step (WS) 2 Half Step (HS) 3 Whole Step (WS) 4 Whole Step (WS) 5.

G minor Pentascale

1. G Major Pentascale is changed to G minor Pentascale by lowering the third note B to _____.

2. Name the notes of the G minor Pentascale: _____, _____, _____, _____, _____.

3. Write the G minor Pentascale Pattern of WS (Whole Steps) and HS (Half Step):

   Steps: 1_____ 2 _____ 3 _____ 4 _____ 5

4. Write the G minor Pentascale in the Bass Clef and the Treble Clef. Use whole notes.
   Name the notes. Draw a line connecting the notes to the keyboard (at the correct pitch).
   Below the staff, draw a square bracket └──┘ for a Whole Step and a slur ◡ for a Half Step.

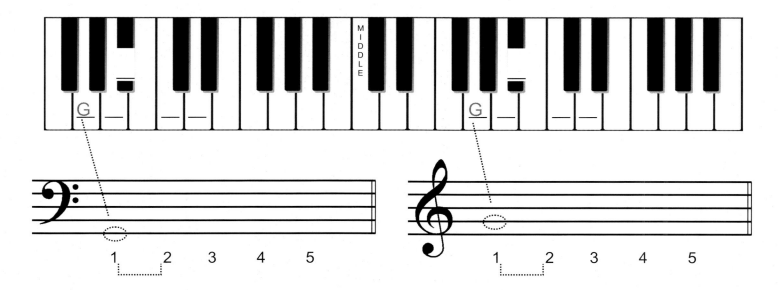

C MAJOR PENTASCALE PATTERN - MAJOR (HAPPY) SOUND

A Pentascale may be a Major (happy) sound or a minor (sad) sound. The difference between the sound of a Major Pentascale and a minor Pentascale is the pattern of whole steps and half step.

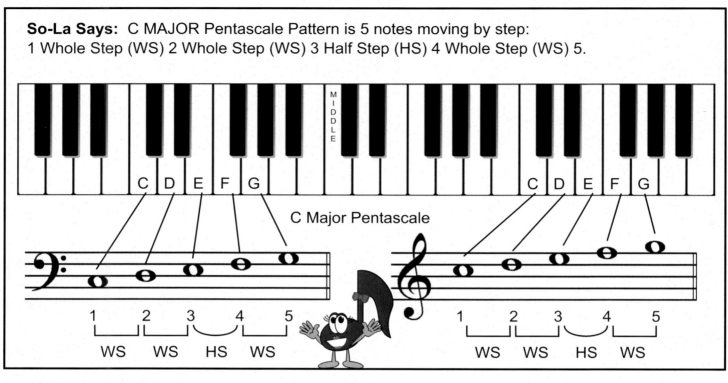

So-La Says: C MAJOR Pentascale Pattern is 5 notes moving by step:
1 Whole Step (WS) 2 Whole Step (WS) 3 Half Step (HS) 4 Whole Step (WS) 5.

C Major Pentascale

1. Difference between a Major and minor Pentascale is the _____ of whole steps and half step.

2. Name the notes of the C Major Pentascale: _____, _____, _____, _____, _____.

3. Write the C Major Pentascale Pattern of WS (Whole Steps) and HS (Half Step):

   Steps: 1_____ 2 _____ 3 _____ 4 _____ 5

4. Write the C Major Pentascale in the Bass Clef and the Treble Clef. Use whole notes.
   Name the notes. Draw a line connecting the notes to the keyboard (at the correct pitch).
   Below the staff, draw a square bracket ⌐⌐ for a Whole Step and a slur ⌣ for a Half Step.

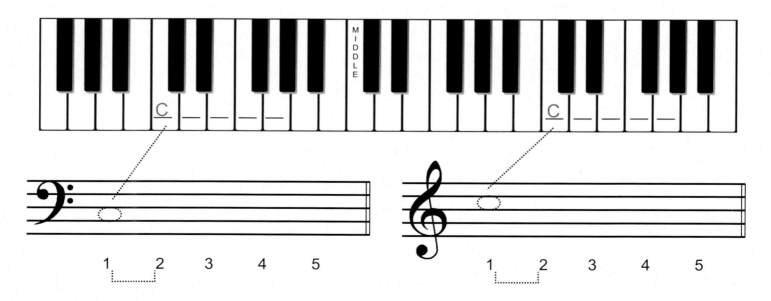

C MINOR PENTASCALE PATTERN - MINOR (SAD) SOUND ☹

C MAJOR Pentascale is changed to C MINOR Pentascale by lowering the third note one half step. The third note E is lowered to E flat. C Major (C, D, E, F, G) to C minor (C, D, E♭, F, G).

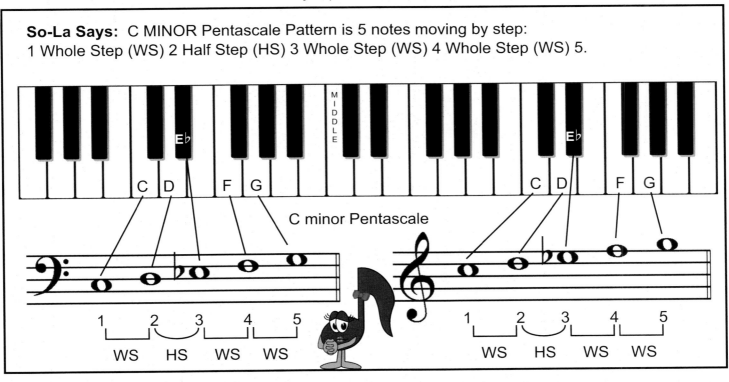

So-La Says: C MINOR Pentascale Pattern is 5 notes moving by step:
1 Whole Step (WS) 2 Half Step (HS) 3 Whole Step (WS) 4 Whole Step (WS) 5.

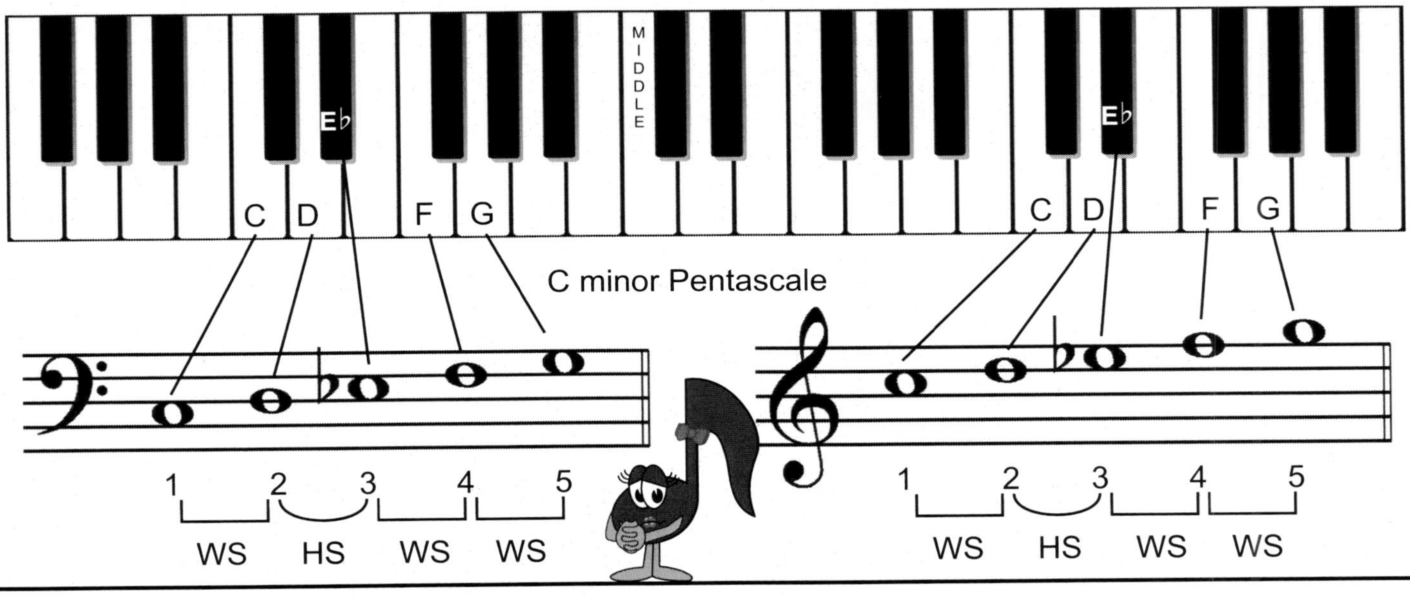

1. C Major Pentascale is changed to C minor Pentascale by lowering the third note E to __________.

2. Name the notes of the C minor Pentascale: ____, ____, ____, ____, ____.

3. Write the C minor Pentascale Pattern of WS (Whole Steps) and HS (Half Step):

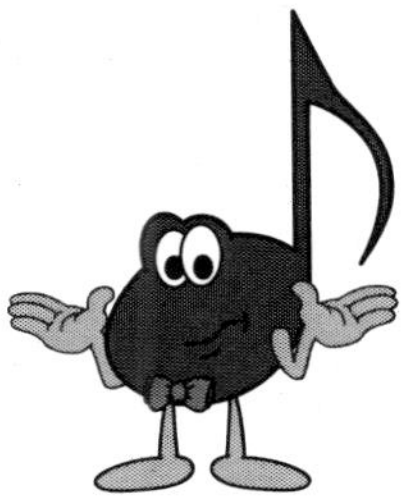

   Steps: 1__________ 2 __________ 3 __________ 4 __________ 5

4. Write the C minor Pentascale in the Bass Clef and the Treble Clef. Use whole notes. Name the notes. Draw a line connecting the notes to the keyboard (at the correct pitch). Below the staff, draw a square bracket ⎣__⎦ for a Whole Step and a slur ◡ for a Half Step.

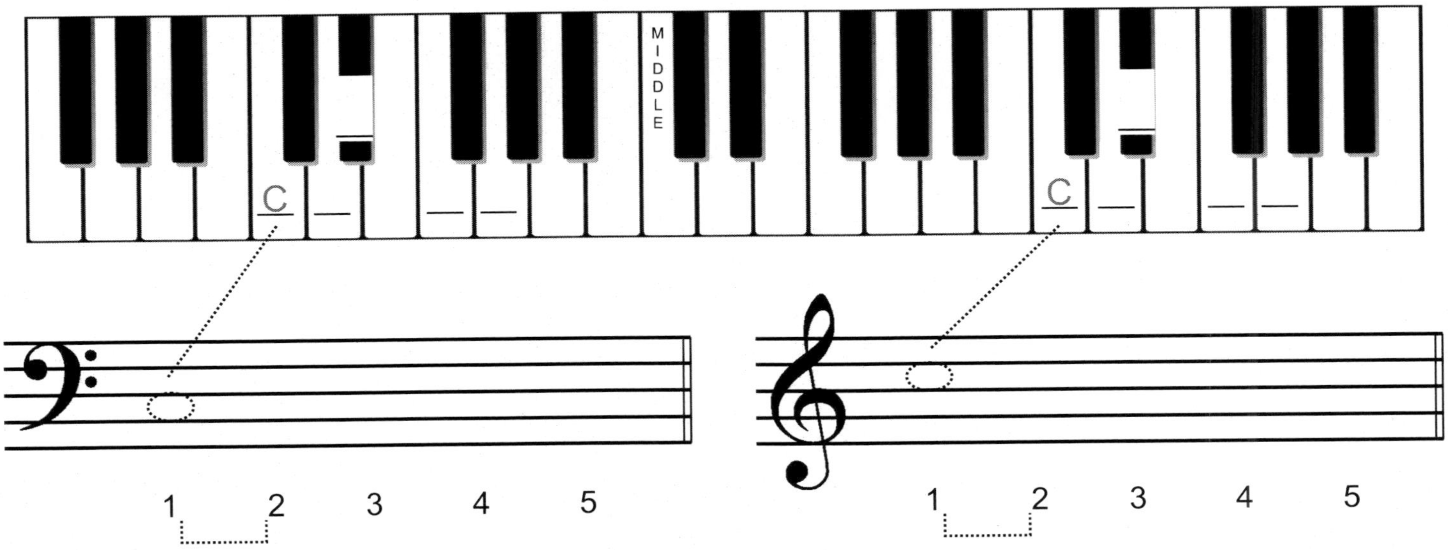

Lesson 7 Review with So-La & Ti-Do

Check:

1. Write the Major Pentascale Pattern of WS (Whole Steps) and HS (Half Step):

   Steps: 1_____ 2 _____ 3 _____ 4 _____ 5   ☺

2. Write the minor Pentascale Pattern of WS (Whole Steps) and HS (Half Step):

   Steps: 1_____ 2 _____ 3 _____ 4 _____ 5   ☹

3. Write the missing note directly on the staff to complete each Pentascale Pattern.
   Use a whole note. Use an accidental (flat) when necessary.
   Draw a line connecting the notes to the keyboard (at the correct pitch).

   a) C Major Pentascale

   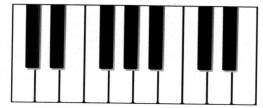

   1   2   3   4   5
   WS WS HS WS

   b) C minor Pentascale

   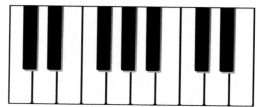

   1   2   3   4   5
   WS HS WS WS

   c) G Major Pentascale

   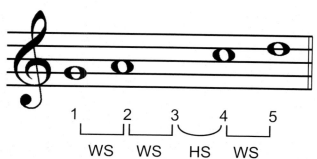

   1   2   3   4   5
   WS WS HS WS

   d) G minor Pentascale

   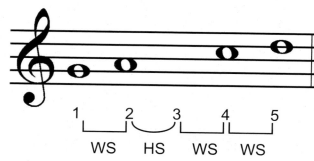

   1   2   3   4   5
   WS HS WS WS

Lesson 7 Review Ultimate Sight Reading & Ear Training Games

1. PLAY "Sweet and Sour Pentascales".
   Below the staff, DRAW a square bracket ⌐_⌐ for a Whole Step and a slur ⌣ for a Half Step.

   DRAW a sweet, happy face ☺ for each Sweet Candy, a Major Pentascale Pattern.

   DRAW a sour, sad face ☹ for each Sour Candy, a minor Pentascale Pattern.

Lesson 8 Pentascale Patterns - D minor/D Major & A minor/A Major

D MINOR PENTASCALE PATTERN - MINOR (SAD) SOUND ☹

So-La Says: D MINOR Pentascale Pattern is 5 notes moving by step:
1 Whole Step (WS) 2 Half Step (HS) 3 Whole Step (WS) 4 Whole Step (WS) 5.

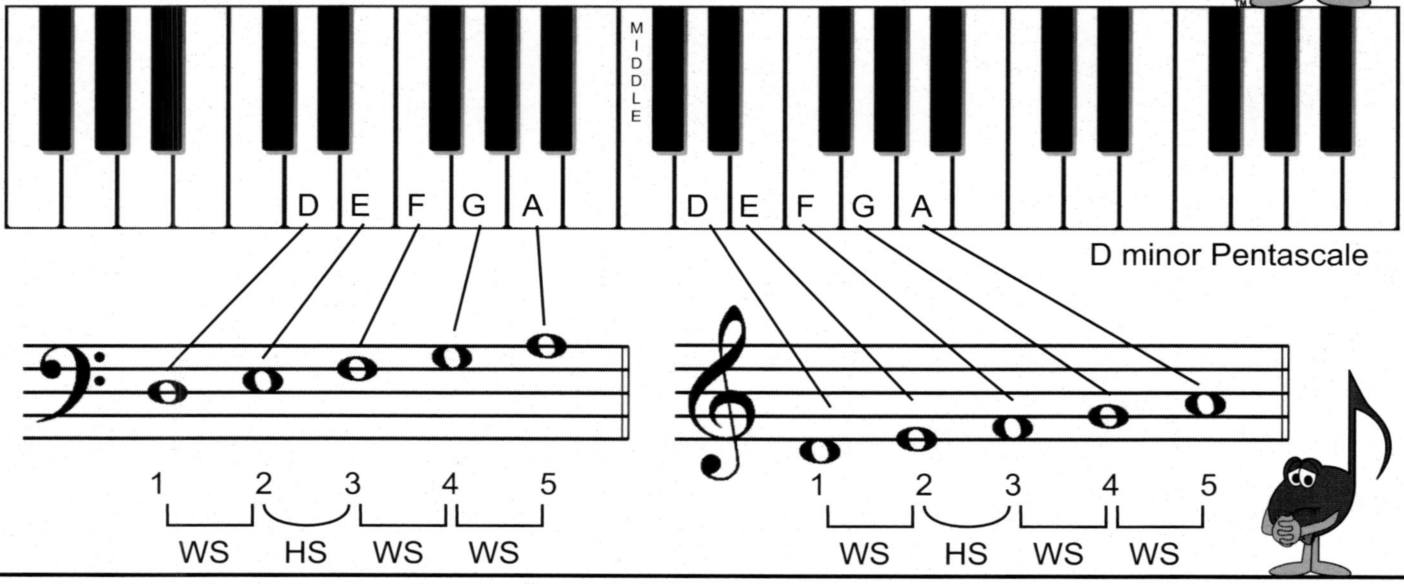

1. The D minor Pentascale pattern is 5 notes moving by __________ and has a __________ sound.

2. Name the notes of the D minor Pentascale: ____, ____, ____, ____, ____.

3. Write the D minor Pentascale Pattern of WS (Whole Steps) and HS (Half Step):

   Steps: 1__________ 2 __________ 3 __________ 4 __________ 5

4. Write the D minor Pentascale in the Bass Clef and the Treble Clef. Use whole notes. Name the notes. Draw a line connecting the notes to the keyboard (at the correct pitch). Below the staff, draw a square bracket ⊔ for a Whole Step and a slur ◡ for a Half Step.

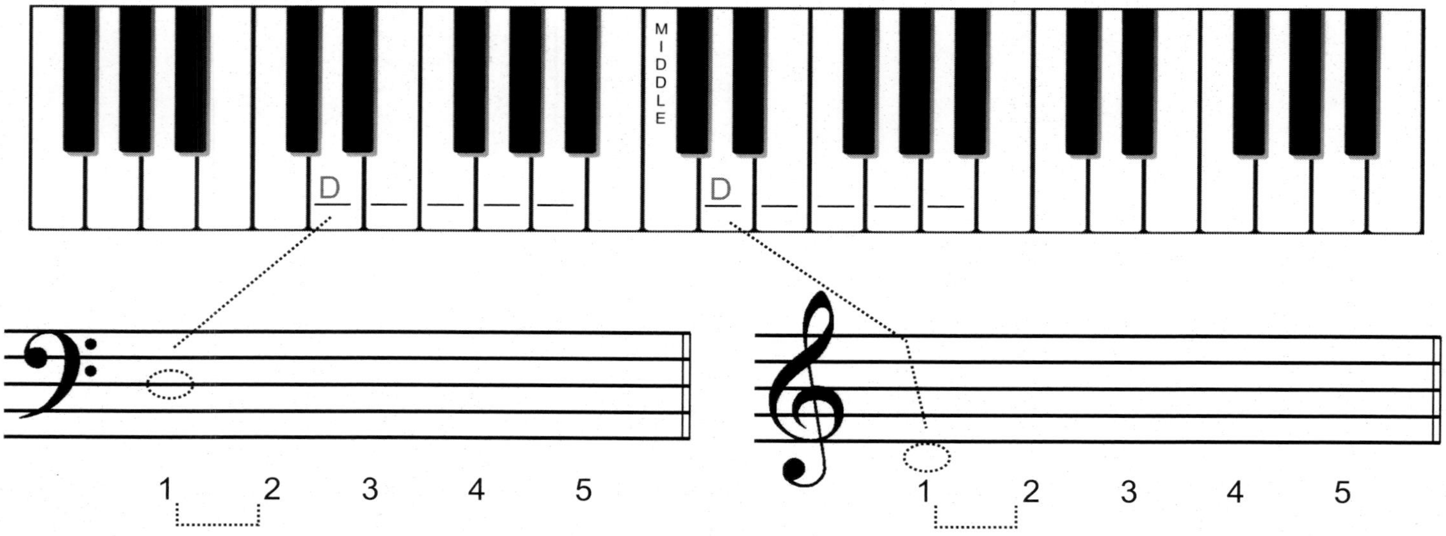

D MAJOR PENTASCALE PATTERN - MAJOR (HAPPY) SOUND

D MINOR Pentascale is changed to D MAJOR Pentascale by raising the third note one half step. The third note F is raised to F sharp. D minor (D, E, F, G, A) to D Major (D, E, F#, G, A).

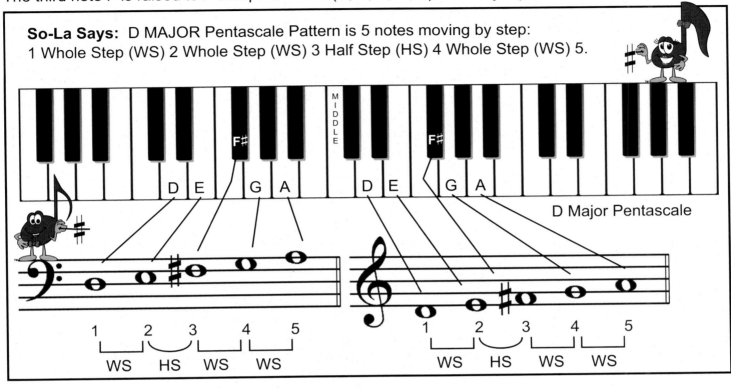

1. D minor Pentascale is changed to D Major Pentascale by raising the third note F to _____.

2. Name the notes of the D Major Pentascale: _____, _____, _____, _____, _____.

3. Write the D Major Pentascale Pattern of WS (Whole Steps) and HS (Half Step):

   Steps: 1_____ 2_____ 3_____ 4_____ 5

4. Write the D Major Pentascale in the Bass Clef and the Treble Clef. Use whole notes.
   Name the notes. Draw a line connecting the notes to the keyboard (at the correct pitch).
   Below the staff, draw a square bracket |___| for a Whole Step and a slur ⌣ for a Half Step.

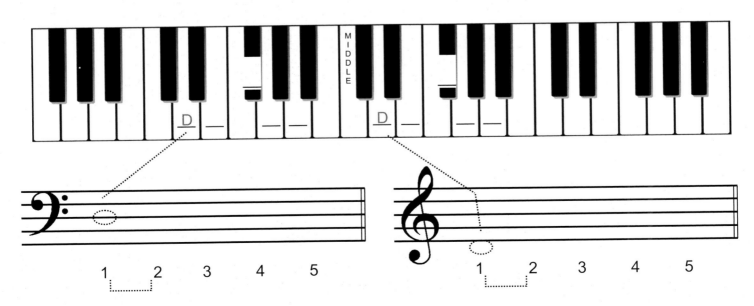

A MINOR PENTASCALE PATTERN - MINOR (SAD) SOUND

A Pentascale may be a Major (happy) sound or a minor (sad) sound. The difference between the sound of a Major Pentascale and a minor Pentascale is the pattern of whole steps and half step.

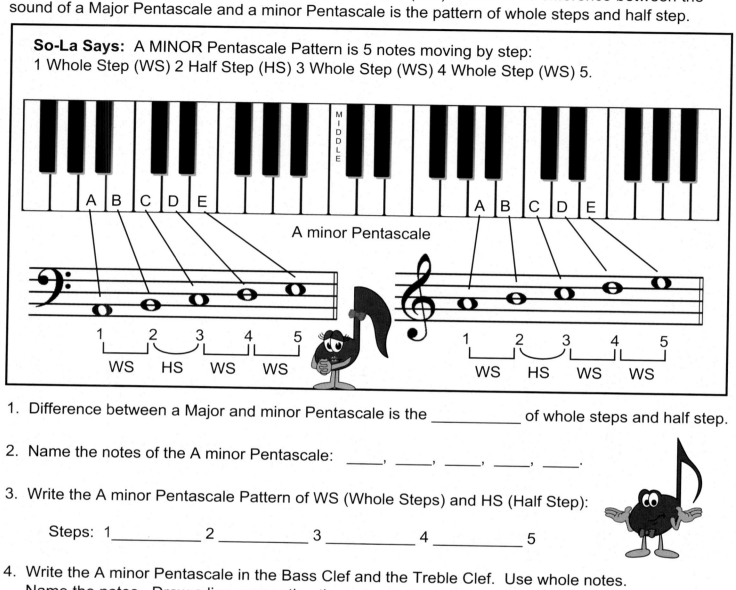

So-La Says: A MINOR Pentascale Pattern is 5 notes moving by step:
1 Whole Step (WS) 2 Half Step (HS) 3 Whole Step (WS) 4 Whole Step (WS) 5.

A minor Pentascale

1. Difference between a Major and minor Pentascale is the _____ of whole steps and half step.

2. Name the notes of the A minor Pentascale: ____, ____, ____, ____, ____.

3. Write the A minor Pentascale Pattern of WS (Whole Steps) and HS (Half Step):

    Steps: 1_____ 2 _____ 3 _____ 4 _____ 5

4. Write the A minor Pentascale in the Bass Clef and the Treble Clef. Use whole notes.
   Name the notes. Draw a line connecting the notes to the keyboard (at the correct pitch).
   Below the staff, draw a square bracket └──┘ for a Whole Step and a slur ⌣ for a Half Step.

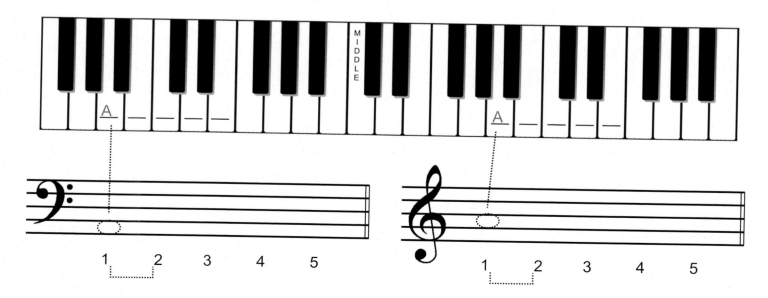

A MAJOR PENTASCALE PATTERN - MAJOR (HAPPY) SOUND

A MINOR Pentascale is changed to A MAJOR Pentascale by raising the third note one half step.
The third note C is raised to C sharp. A minor (A, B, C, D, E) to A Major (A, B, C#, D, E).

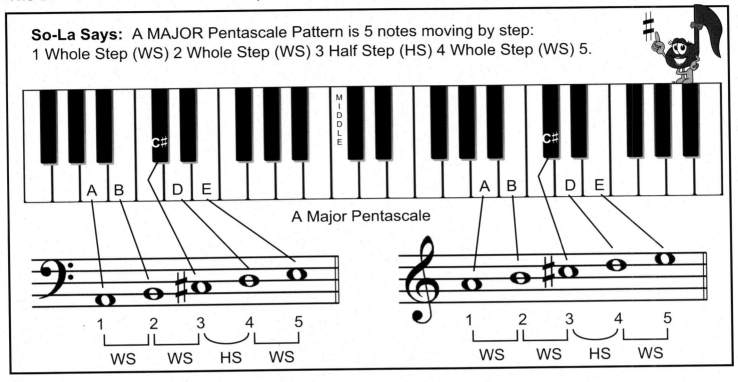

So-La Says: A MAJOR Pentascale Pattern is 5 notes moving by step:
1 Whole Step (WS) 2 Whole Step (WS) 3 Half Step (HS) 4 Whole Step (WS) 5.

A Major Pentascale

1. A minor Pentascale is changed to A Major Pentascale by raising the third note C to _____.

2. Name the notes of the A Major Pentascale: ____, ____, ____, ____, ____.

3. Write the A Major Pentascale Pattern of WS (Whole Steps) and HS (Half Step):

   Steps: 1_____ 2 _____ 3 _____ 4 _____ 5

4. Write the A Major Pentascale in the Bass Clef and the Treble Clef. Use whole notes.
   Name the notes. Draw a line connecting the notes to the keyboard (at the correct pitch).
   Below the staff, draw a square bracket ⌐⌐ for a Whole Step and a slur ⌣ for a Half Step.

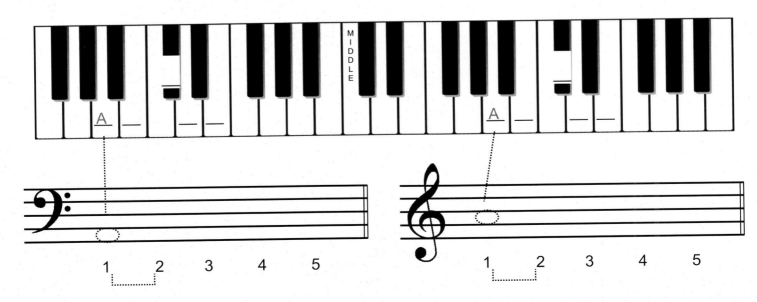

Lesson 8 Review with So-La & Ti-Do

Check:

1. Write the Major Pentascale Pattern of WS (Whole Steps) and HS (Half Step):

    Steps: 1_____ 2 _____ 3 _____ 4 _____ 5

2. Write the minor Pentascale Pattern of WS (Whole Steps) and HS (Half Step):

    Steps: 1_____ 2 _____ 3 _____ 4 _____ 5

3. Write the missing note directly on the staff to complete each Pentascale Pattern.
    Use a whole note. Use an accidental (sharp) when necessary.
    Draw a line connecting the notes to the keyboard (at the correct pitch).

a) D Major Pentascale

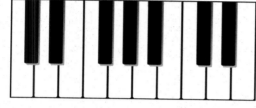

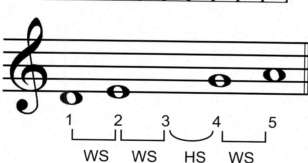

b) D minor Pentascale

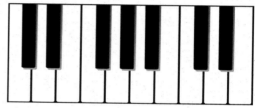

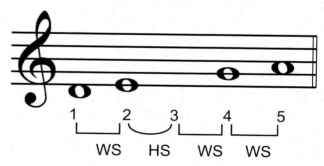

c) A Major Pentascale

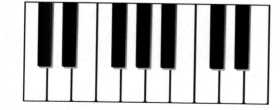

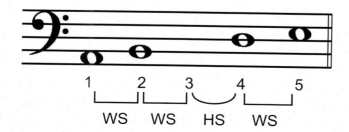

d) A minor Pentascale

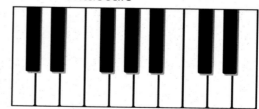

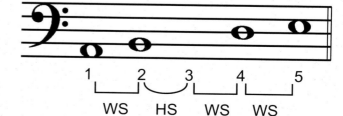

Lesson 8 Review Ultimate Sight Reading & Ear Training Games

1. PLAY "Happy Major Pentascale or Sad Minor Pentascale".
   Below the staff, DRAW a square bracket ⌐⌐ for a Whole Step and a slur ◡ for a Half Step.

   On the piano, PLAY each Pentascale.
   CIRCLE "Happy Major Pentascale" if the Pentascale Pattern is Major.
   CIRCLE "Sad minor Pentascale" if the Pentascale Pattern is minor.

a)

1 2 3 4 5

Happy Major ☺   or   Sad minor ☹
Pentascale   Pentascale

b)

1 2 3 4 5

Happy Major ☺   or   Sad minor ☹
Pentascale   Pentascale

c)

1 2 3 4 5

Happy Major ☺   or   Sad minor ☹
Pentascale   Pentascale

d)

1 2 3 4 5

Happy Major ☺   or   Sad minor ☹
Pentascale   Pentascale

e)

1 2 3 4 5

Happy Major ☺   or   Sad minor ☹
Pentascale   Pentascale

f)

1 2 3 4 5

Happy Major ☺   or   Sad minor ☹
Pentascale   Pentascale

g)

1 2 3 4 5

Happy Major ☺   or   Sad minor ☹
Pentascale   Pentascale

h)

1 2 3 4 5

Happy Major ☺   or   Sad minor ☹
Pentascale   Pentascale

Lesson 9   Types of Notes and Note Values

TYPES OF NOTES - WHOLE, HALF, QUARTER and EIGHTH NOTES

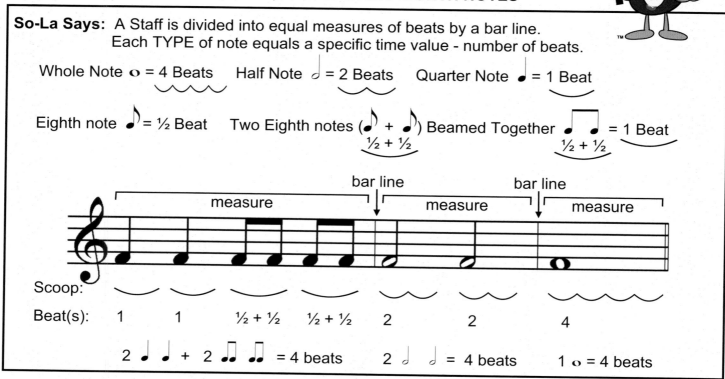

So-La Says: A Staff is divided into equal measures of beats by a bar line.
Each TYPE of note equals a specific time value - number of beats.

Whole Note 𝅝 = 4 Beats   Half Note 𝅗𝅥 = 2 Beats   Quarter Note ♩ = 1 Beat

Eighth note ♪ = ½ Beat   Two Eighth notes (♪ + ♪) Beamed Together ♫ = 1 Beat
                            ½ + ½   ½ + ½

Scoop:

Beat(s):   1   1   ½ + ½   ½ + ½   2   2   4

2 ♩ ♩ + 2 ♫ ♫ = 4 beats   2 𝅗𝅥 𝅗𝅥 = 4 beats   1 𝅝 = 4 beats

♫ **Ti-Do Tip:** One scoop ⌣ is a symbol for one beat. 1 scoop = 1 beat

1. Draw the correct number of scoops below each type of note(s). Write the number of beats below.
   Name the notes. Play each melody on the piano.

Scoop:

Beat(s):   1   ___ ___ + ___ ___ + ___ ___ ___

Notes: G   ___ ___ ___ ___ ___ ___

Scoop:

Beat(s):   ½ + ½ ___ + ___ ___ ___ ___ ___ ___

Notes: G   B   ___ ___ ___ ___ ___ ___

NOTE VALUES - WHOLE, HALF, QUARTER and EIGHTH NOTES

Different TYPES of notes have different NOTE VALUES - specific number of beats.

Eighth Notes 𝅘𝅥𝅮𝅘𝅥𝅮 also called a "ti ti" = 1 beat of sound, 1 scoop = 4 Beats
ti ti ti ti ti ti ti ti

Quarter Note ♩ also called a "ta" = 1 beat of sound, 1 scoop = 4 Beats
ta ta ta ta

Half Note 𝅗𝅥 = 2 beats of sound, 2 scoops connected = 4 Beats
half note half note

Whole Note 𝅝 = 4 beats of sound, 4 scoops connected = 4 Beats
great big whole note

1. Fill in the blanks for each type of note and the number of beats for each.

Type of note 𝅘𝅥𝅮𝅘𝅥𝅮 _____ notes also called a "_____" = ___ beat of sound ⌣

Type of note ♩ _____ note also called a "_____" = ___ beat of sound ⌣

Type of note 𝅗𝅥 _____ note = ___ beats of sound ⌣⌣   (𝅗𝅥 = half note)

Type of note 𝅝 _____ note = ___ beats of sound ⌣⌣⌣

2. Add scoops (one for each beat) below the following notes.

𝅘𝅥𝅮𝅘𝅥𝅮   ♩   𝅗𝅥   𝅝   𝅘𝅥𝅮𝅘𝅥𝅮   ♩   𝅗𝅥   𝅝
ti ti ta half note great big whole note ti ti ta half note great big whole note

3. Name the type of note as: whole, half, quarter or eighth notes. Write the number of beats for each.

Type: _quarter_ _____ _____ _____ _____ _____

Beat(s): _1_ _____ _____ _____ _____ _____

Type: _whole_ _____ _____ _____ _____ _____

Beat(s): _4_ _____ _____ _____ _____ _____

TREBLE CLEF - WRITING WHOLE, HALF, QUARTER and EIGHTH NOTES

Whole Note has a circle called a notehead. Half Note has a line on the side of the notehead called a stem. Quarter Note has a black notehead. Eighth note stems are connected by a beam.

As seen in music:

Notehead   Stem   Black   Beam

Whole   Half   Quarter   Eighth

As drawn by hand:

Notehead   Stem   Black   Beam

Whole   Half   Quarter   Eighth

Treble Clef - Middle C up to B on line 3, the stem direction is up on the RIGHT of the notehead. A stem length crosses 3 lines and 3 spaces. The eighth note beam is at the end of the stems.

1. Draw a Treble Clef at the beginning of each staff. Write notes in each measure to equal 4 beats.

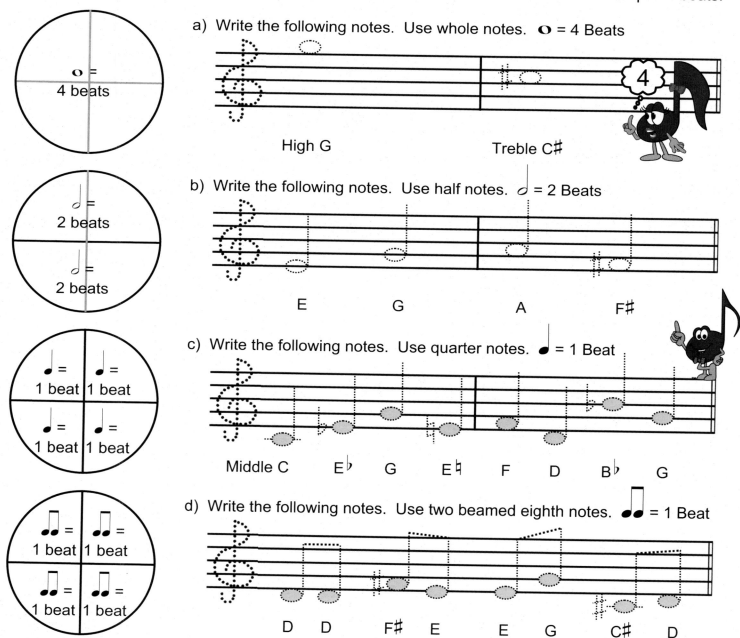

a) Write the following notes. Use whole notes. 𝅝 = 4 Beats

High G   Treble C♯

b) Write the following notes. Use half notes. 𝅗𝅥 = 2 Beats

E   G   A   F♯

c) Write the following notes. Use quarter notes. ♩ = 1 Beat

Middle C   E♭   G   E♮   F   D   B♭   G

d) Write the following notes. Use two beamed eighth notes. ♫ = 1 Beat

D   D   F♯   E   E   G   C♯   D

BASS CLEF - WRITING WHOLE, HALF, QUARTER and EIGHTH NOTES

Whole Note has a circle called a notehead. Half Note has a line on the side of the notehead called a stem. Quarter Note has a black notehead. Eighth note stems are connected by a beam.

As seen in music:
Notehead   Stem   Black   Beam

Whole   Half   Quarter   Eighth

As drawn by hand:
Notehead   Stem   Black   Beam

Whole   Half   Quarter   Eighth

Bass Clef - Middle C down to D line 3, the stem direction is down on the LEFT of the notehead. A stem length crosses 3 lines and 3 spaces. The eighth note beam is at the end of the stems.

1. Draw a Bass Clef at the beginning of each staff. Write notes in each measure to equal 4 beats.

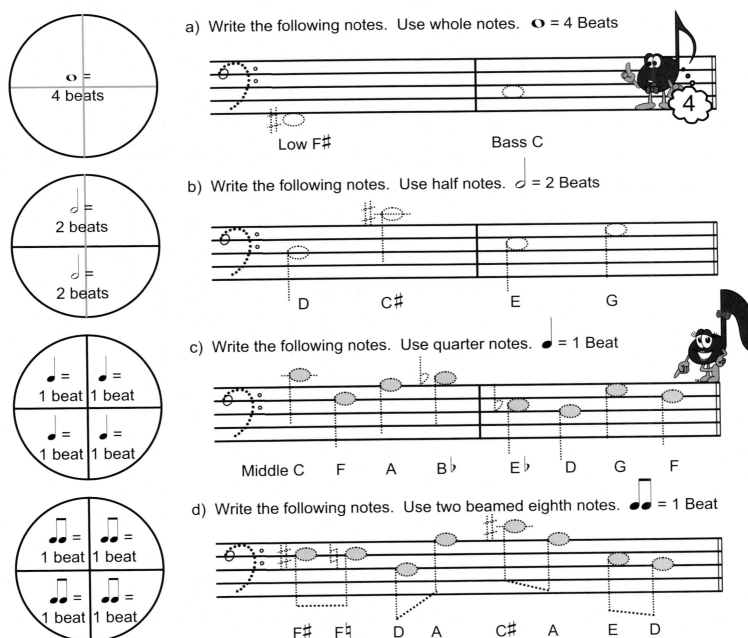

a) Write the following notes. Use whole notes. 𝐨 = 4 Beats

Low F#   Bass C

b) Write the following notes. Use half notes. ♩ = 2 Beats

D   C#   E   G

c) Write the following notes. Use quarter notes. ♩ = 1 Beat

Middle C   F   A   B♭   E♭   D   G   F

d) Write the following notes. Use two beamed eighth notes. ♫ = 1 Beat

F#   F♮   D   A   C#   A   E   D

Lesson 9 Review with So-La & Ti-Do

Check:

1. Draw the correct number of scoops below each note. Write the number of beats below each note. Name the notes. Play the melody on the piano.

Scoop:

Beat(s): ½ + ½ ___ + ___ ___ ___ ___ ___

Notes: C D ___ ___ ___ ___ ___ ___

2. Write the number of beats below each scoop. Name the notes.
Below each bracket, write the missing note(s) in each measure. Use the correct note name and the correct note value. Play each melody on the piano.

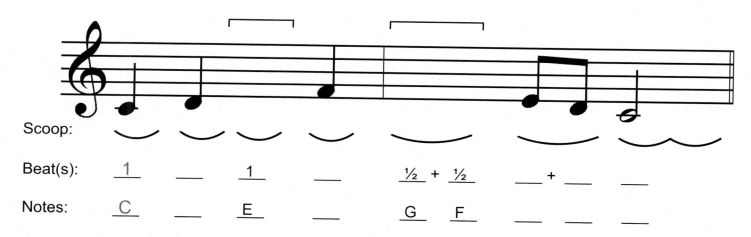

Scoop:

Beat(s): 1 ___ 1 ___ ½ + ½ ___ + ___ ___

Notes: C ___ E ___ G F ___ ___ ___

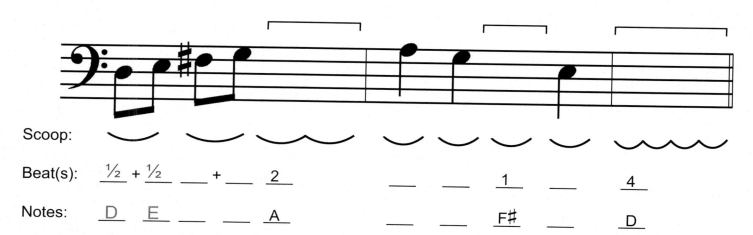

Scoop:

Beat(s): ½ + ½ ___ + ___ 2 ___ ___ 1 ___ 4

Notes: D E ___ ___ A ___ ___ F♯ ___ D

Lesson 9 Review Ultimate Sight Reading & Ear Training Games

1. Play "Rhythm Drum Math"!
   WRITE the number of beats below each note.
   ADD the note values together and write the Total Beats in each Drum.

   LISTEN as your Teacher CLAPS (TAPS) the notes in a Drum. Color the Drum Stick
   with the correct rhythm (note value pattern).

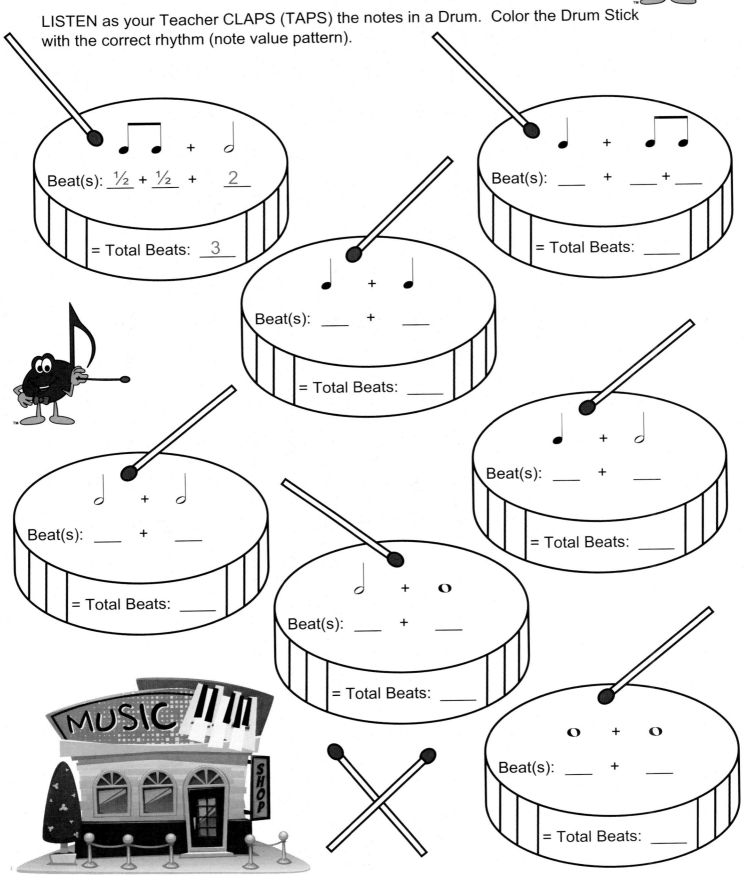

Beat(s): ½ + ½ + 2

= Total Beats: 3

Beat(s): ___ + ___ + ___

= Total Beats: ____

Beat(s): ___ + ___

= Total Beats: ____

Beat(s): ___ + ___

= Total Beats: ____

Beat(s): ___ + ___

= Total Beats: ____

Beat(s): ___ + ___

= Total Beats: ____

Beat(s): ___ + ___

= Total Beats: ____

Lesson 10   Time Signature - Notes & Rest Values

TIME SIGNATURE - NUMBER OF EQUAL BEATS PER MEASURE

A Time Signature is written on the staff after the clef. Time Signature $\frac{4}{4}$ is Simple Time.

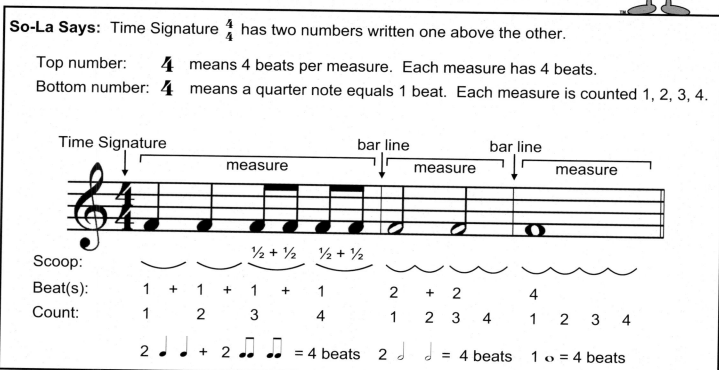

So-La Says: Time Signature $\frac{4}{4}$ has two numbers written one above the other.

Top number: **4** means 4 beats per measure. Each measure has 4 beats.

Bottom number: **4** means a quarter note equals 1 beat. Each measure is counted 1, 2, 3, 4.

♫ **Ti-Do Tip:** In $\frac{4}{4}$ time, each measure contains 4 beats. One quarter note equals 1 beat = 1 scoop.

1. Draw the correct number of scoops below each note.
    Write the counts (1, 2, 3, 4) below the scoops in each measure.

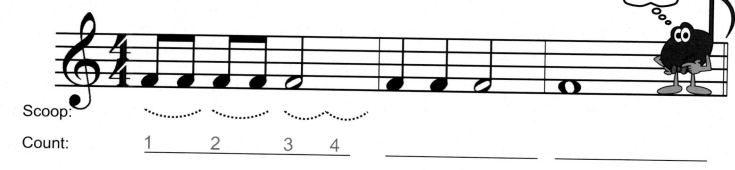

TIME SIGNATURE - RHYTHM and REST VALUES - WHOLE, HALF and QUARTER RESTS

TIME SIGNATURE $\frac{4}{4}$ indicates 4 beats per measure. Each beat may be a note value of sound or a rest value of silence. Rhythm is different types of notes (sound) or rests (silence) in each measure.

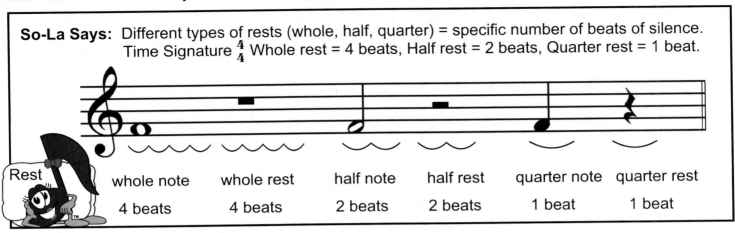

So-La Says: Different types of rests (whole, half, quarter) = specific number of beats of silence.
Time Signature $\frac{4}{4}$ Whole rest = 4 beats, Half rest = 2 beats, Quarter rest = 1 beat.

whole note	whole rest	half note	half rest	quarter note	quarter rest
4 beats	4 beats	2 beats	2 beats	1 beat	1 beat

♫ **Ti-Do Tip:** Rests are written in the SAME place in the Treble Clef and in the Bass Clef.

1. Name the type of note or rest (whole, half, quarter). Write the number of beat(s) for each.

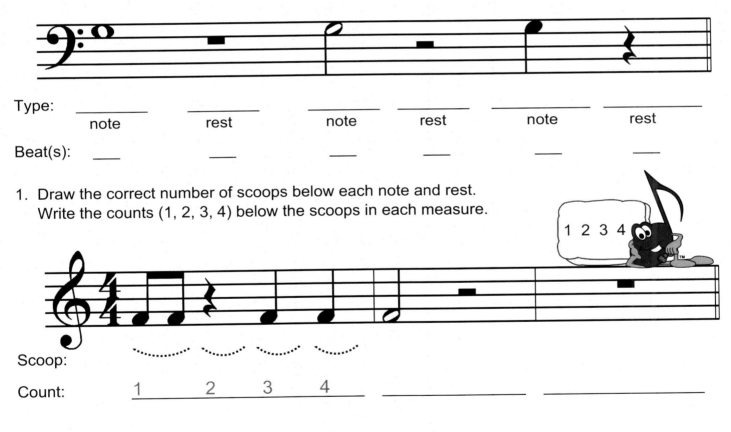

Type: _____   _____   _____   _____   _____   _____
        note   rest   note   rest   note   rest

Beat(s): ___   ___   ___   ___   ___   ___

1. Draw the correct number of scoops below each note and rest.
   Write the counts (1, 2, 3, 4) below the scoops in each measure.

1 2 3 4

Scoop:

Count: 1   2   3   4   _____   _____

Scoop:

Count: 1 2 3 4   _____   _____

TIME SIGNATURE - ADDING BAR LINES

In $\frac{4}{4}$ time, the rhythm in each measure equals 4 beats. Each measure is divided by a BAR LINE.

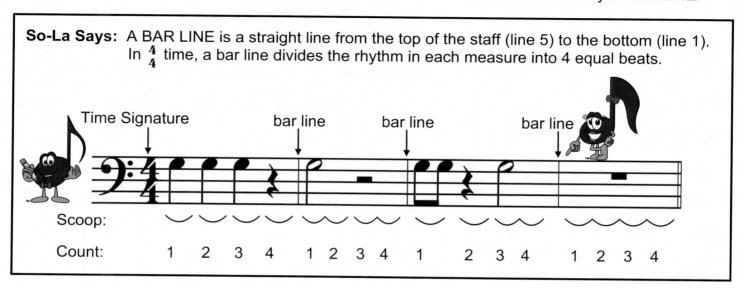

So-La Says: A BAR LINE is a straight line from the top of the staff (line 5) to the bottom (line 1). In $\frac{4}{4}$ time, a bar line divides the rhythm in each measure into 4 equal beats.

Time Signature   bar line   bar line   bar line

Scoop:

Count: 1 2 3 4   1 2 3 4   1   2   3   4   1 2 3 4

♫ **Ti-Do Tip:** Use a ruler to draw straight bar lines on the staff from the top line 5 down to line 1.

1. The Time Signature is $\frac{4}{4}$. Add bar lines to divide the staff into equal measures of 4 beats.

Count: 1 2 3 4   1   2   3 4   1 2   3   4   1   2 3 4

2. Write the counts (1, 2, 3, 4) below the notes. Add bar lines to create equal measures in $\frac{4}{4}$ time.

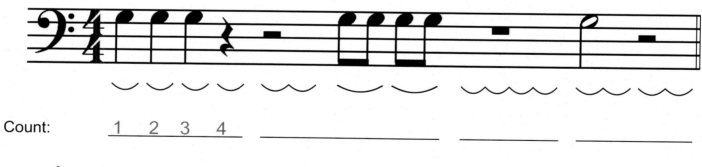

Count: 1 2 3 4 _____ _____ _____

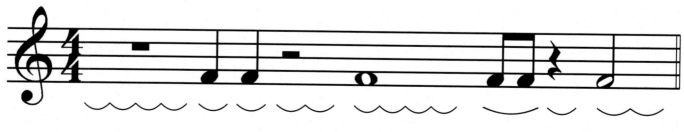

Count: 1 2 3 4 _____ _____ _____

TIME SIGNATURE - ADDING REST VALUES

In $\frac{4}{4}$ time, the note and rest values in each measure equal 4 beats. Each type of rest has a VALUE.

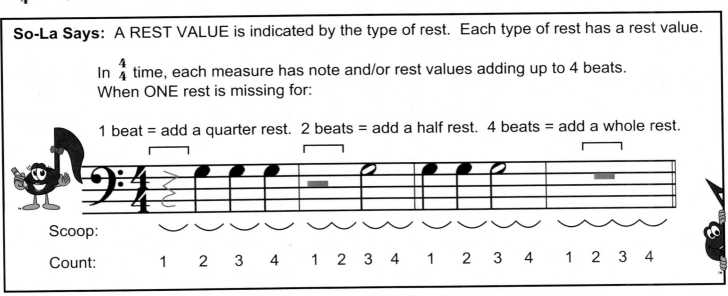

So-La Says: A REST VALUE is indicated by the type of rest. Each type of rest has a rest value.

In $\frac{4}{4}$ time, each measure has note and/or rest values adding up to 4 beats.
When ONE rest is missing for:

1 beat = add a quarter rest. 2 beats = add a half rest. 4 beats = add a whole rest.

Scoop:

Count: 1 2 3 4   1 2 3 4   1 2 3 4   1 2 3 4

♫ **Ti-Do Tip:** Count the number of beats in each measure to determine the missing rest value.

1. The Time Signature is $\frac{4}{4}$. Add one rest below each bracket to create equal measures of 4 beats.

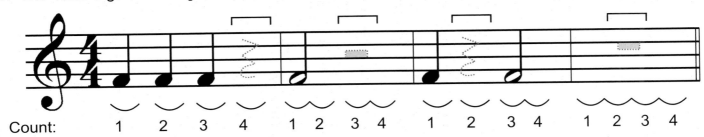

Count: 1 2 3 4   1 2 3 4   1 2 3 4   1 2 3 4

2. Write the counts (1, 2, 3, 4) below each measure. Add one rest to create equal measures in $\frac{4}{4}$ time.

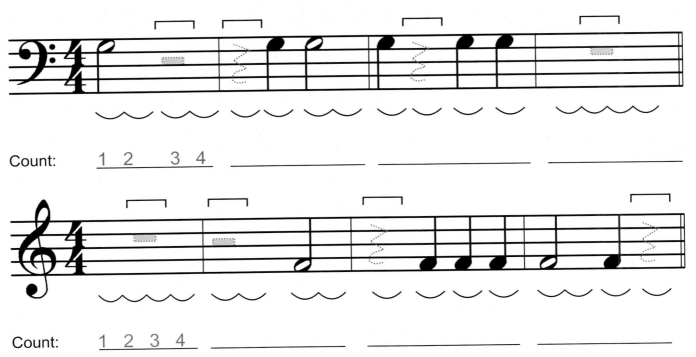

Count: 1 2 3 4 _____ _____ _____

Count: 1 2 3 4 _____ _____ _____

TREBLE CLEF and BASS CLEF - WRITING $\frac{4}{4}$ TIME SIGNATURE

So-La Says: A Time Signature is two numbers (one above the other). A Time Signature is written in the SAME place on the staff for both Treble Clef and Bass Clef.

As seen in music:
Time Signature

As drawn by hand:
Time Signature

$\frac{4}{4} = \frac{4}{4}$

4 Top number means 4 beats per measure.
4 Bottom number means a quarter note equals 1 beat.

Each 4 uses 2 spaces.

♫ **Ti-Do Tip:** In $\frac{4}{4}$ Time Signature, a whole rest equals 4 beats of silence. A whole rest is written in the MIDDLE of the measure.

1. In $\frac{4}{4}$ Time, the two numbers are written in the _____ place for both Treble Clef and Bass Clef.

Top number means ____ beats per measure. Bottom number means a quarter note equals ___ beat.

2. In $\frac{4}{4}$ Time, a whole rest equals ____ beats and is written in the _____ of the measure.

3. For each melody: Add the Time Signature $\frac{4}{4}$ below the bracket. Name the notes. Write the counts below each measure. Play each melody on the piano. Observe the rests. Count out loud.

Notes: E♭   __ __ __   __ __ __ __   __ __ __ __ __

Count: 1 2 3   4   _____   _____

Notes: __ __ __ __   __ __ __   __ __ __ __ __

Count: _____   _____   __ __ __ __ __

TREBLE CLEF and BASS CLEF - WRITING WHOLE, HALF and QUARTER RESTS

So-La Says: Different Types of Rests are written in specific places on the staff. Each type of rest is written in the SAME place on the staff for both Treble Clef and Bass Clef.

As seen in music:

Whole   Half   Quarter

As drawn by hand:

Whole   Half   Quarter

Whole rest ▬ hangs from line 4 and takes up half of space 3.

Half rest ▬ sits on line 3 and takes up half of space 3.

Quarter rest ⁊ begins in space 4 and ends in space 1. (Z with a c)

1. Fill in the blanks for each type of rest and the number of beats for each.

Type of rest ⁊ _____ rest = ___ beat of silence

Type of rest ▬ _____ rest = ___ beats of silence

Type of rest ▬ _____ rest = ___ beats of silence

Shhh… Silence

Rest

2. For each melody: Add one rest below each bracket. Use the correct rest value (quarter, half or whole). Name the notes. Play the melody on the piano. Observe the rests. Count out loud.

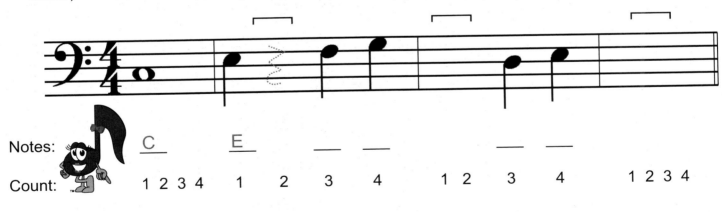

Notes: C ___ E ___ ___ ___ ___ ___

Count: 1 2 3 4   1   2   3   4   1 2   3   4   1 2 3 4

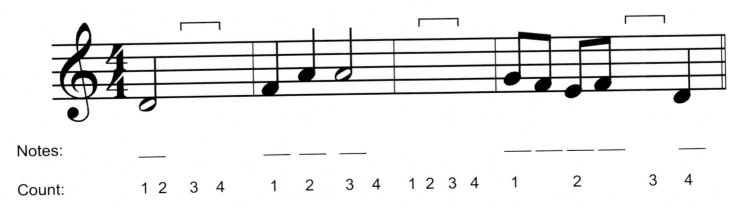

Notes: ___   ___ ___ ___   ___ ___ ___   ___

Count: 1 2   3   4   1   2   3   4 1 2 3 4   1   2   3   4

Lesson 10 Review with So-La & Ti-Do

Check:

1. Write the counts (1, 2, 3, 4) below the notes/rests. Add bar lines to create equal measures of 4. Play each melody on the piano. Observe the note and rest values. Count out loud.

Count: 1   2   3   4

Count: 1   2   3   4

2. Write the 4/4 Time Signature at the beginning of each of the following melodies, after the Clef sign. Add one rest below each bracket. Use the correct rest value (quarter, half or whole). Play each melody on the piano. Observe the note and rest values. Count out loud.

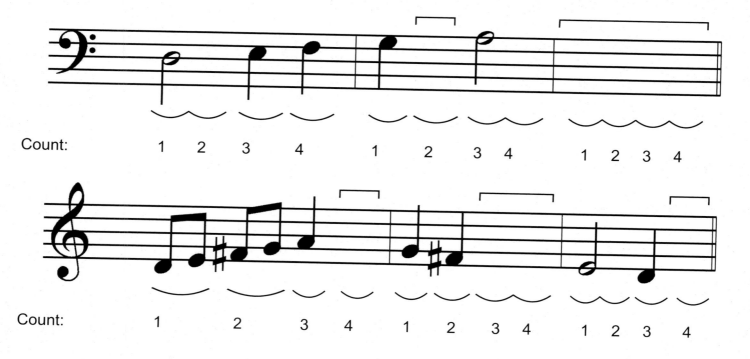

Count: 1   2   3   4   1   2   3   4   1   2   3   4

Count: 1   2   3   4   1   2   3   4   1   2   3   4

Lesson 10 Review Ultimate Sight Reading & Ear Training Games

1. Eating Pizza! Each Pizza is divided into 4 pieces.
    WRITE the missing rest(s) and beat(s) to show how many pieces of pizza were eaten.

    1 piece of pizza eaten = 1 beat - 1 quarter rest

    2 pieces of pizza eaten = 2 beats - 1 half rest

    4 pieces of pizza eaten = 4 beats - 1 whole rest

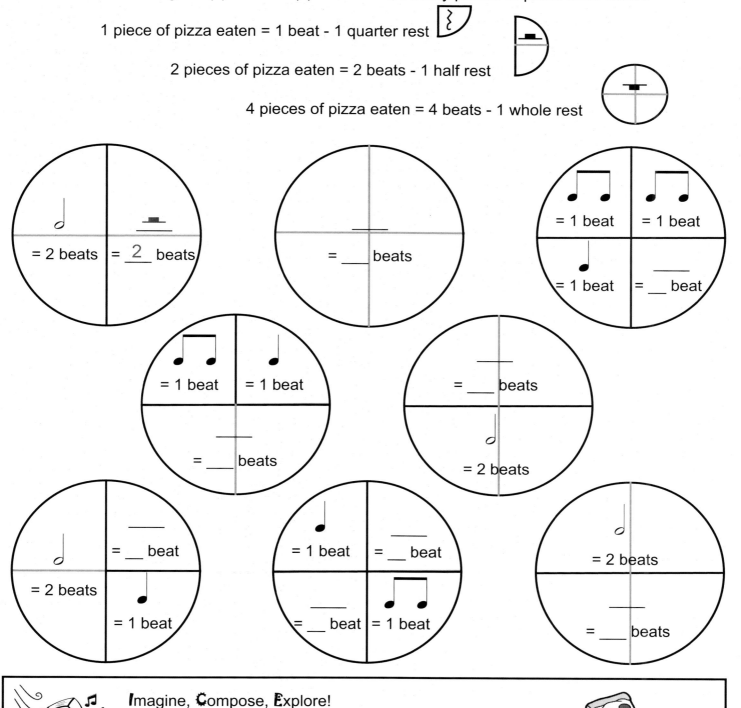

Lesson 11   Pentascales and Pentascale Melodies

PENTASCALES - MAJOR (HAPPY) SOUND, MINOR (SAD) SOUND

Pentascales are a 5 note pattern moving by Whole Steps (WS) and Half Step (HS).
Pentascale Patterns - MAJOR: WS, WS, HS, WS and MINOR: WS, HS, WS, WS.

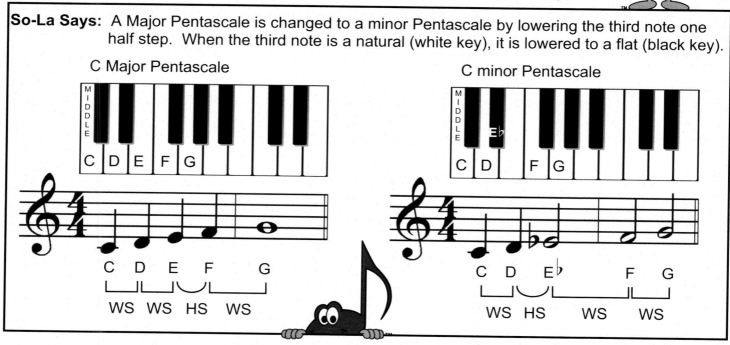

1. Name the following Pentascales as: G Major, G minor, C Major or C minor. Name the notes.
Name the steps as WS for Whole Step and HS for Half Step. Play each Pentascale on the piano.

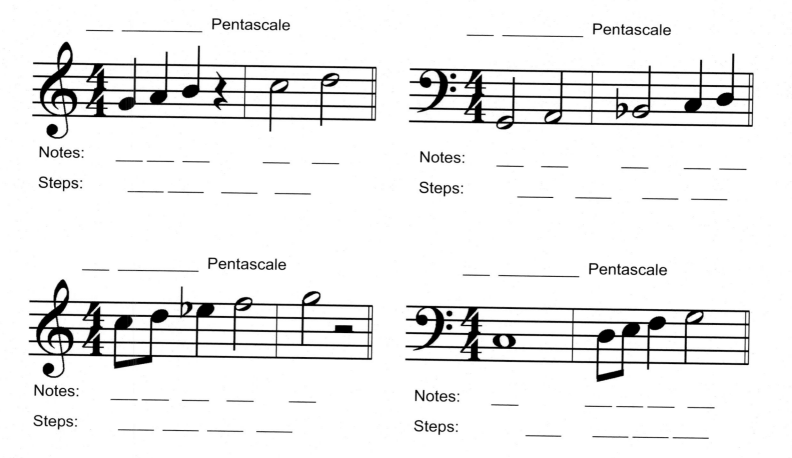

PENTASCALES and RHYTHM

A melody may be written based on the notes of a Major Pentascale or a minor Pentascale. A melody has a rhythm (different note and rest values) divided into equal measures separated by a bar line.

In $\frac{4}{4}$ Time, each measure has 4 beats. Different rhythms may be used to write and play Pentascales.

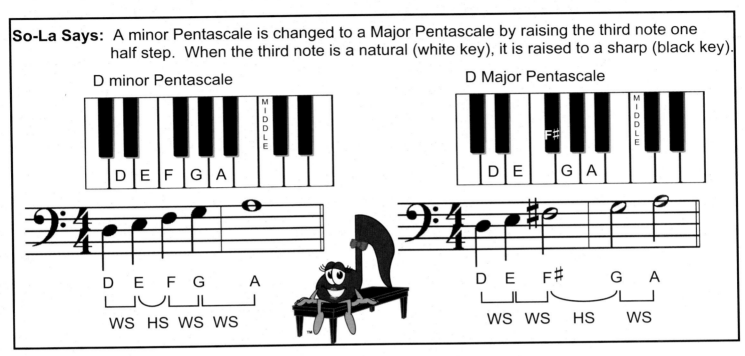

So-La Says: A minor Pentascale is changed to a Major Pentascale by raising the third note one half step. When the third note is a natural (white key), it is raised to a sharp (black key).

D minor Pentascale

D E F G A
WS HS WS WS

D Major Pentascale

D E F♯ G A
WS WS HS WS

1. Name the following Pentascales as: D Major, D minor, A Major or A minor. Name the notes. Name the steps as WS for Whole Step and HS for Half Step. Play each Pentascale on the piano.

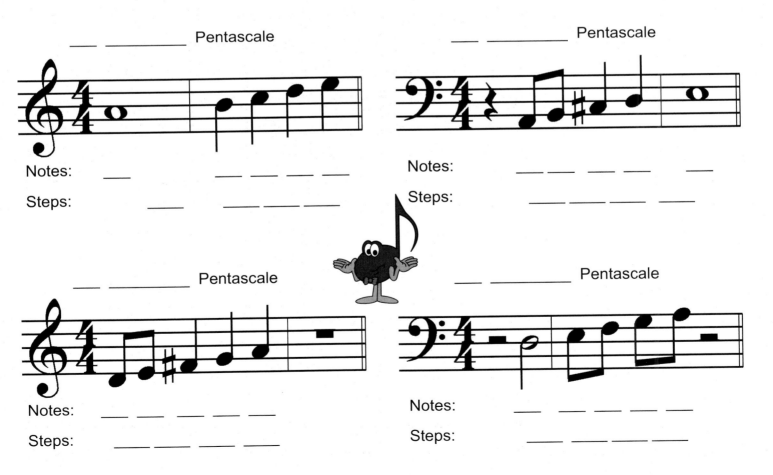

____ _____ Pentascale

Notes: ___ ___ ___ ___ ___

Steps: ____ ____ ____ ____

____ _____ Pentascale

Notes: ___ ___ ___ ___ ___

Steps: ____ ____ ____ ____

____ _____ Pentascale

Notes: ___ ___ ___ ___ ___

Steps: ____ ____ ____ ____

____ _____ Pentascale

Notes: ___ ___ ___ ___ ___

Steps: ____ ____ ____ ____

PENTASCALE MELODIES - G MAJOR (HAPPY) and G MINOR (SAD)

A melody has the same number of beats in each measure, as indicated by the TIME SIGNATURE.

So-La Says: A melody may be written based on the 5 notes of the G Major or G minor Pentascale.

Time Signature $\frac{4}{4}$ Top number, 4 beats per measure. Bottom number, quarter note equals 1 count.

Time Signature   Pentascale melody: G Major

Notes: G B D   C B A B   G B D   G

Count: 1 2 3 4   1 2 3 4   1 2 3 4   1 2 3 4

1. Name the Pentascale notes: G Major ___, ___, ___, ___, ___. G minor ___, ___, ___, ___, ___.

2. In $\frac{4}{4}$ Time: Top number, ___ beats per measure. Bottom number, quarter note equals ___ count.

3. Add the correct Time Signature below each bracket to indicate four beats in each measure.
   For each melody: Name the notes. Write the counts below each measure. Play each melody.
   Name the Pentascale melody as: G Major or G minor.

Pentascale melody: ___ _____

Notes: __ __ __ __   __ __ __ __   __ __ __ __

Count: _____ _____ _____ _____

Pentascale melody: ___ _____

Notes: __ __   __ __ __   __ __ __   __

Count: _____ _____ _____ _____

PENTASCALE MELODIES - C MAJOR (HAPPY) and C MINOR (SAD)

A melody is written with rhythms (notes and/or rests) divided into equal measures by a BAR LINE.

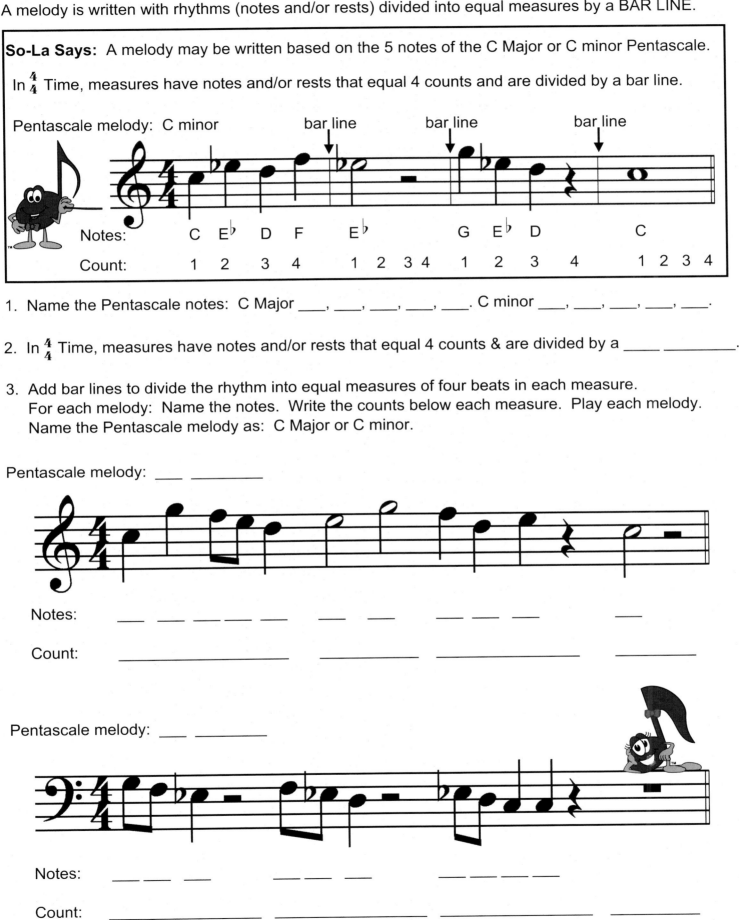

So-La Says: A melody may be written based on the 5 notes of the C Major or C minor Pentascale.

In $\frac{4}{4}$ Time, measures have notes and/or rests that equal 4 counts and are divided by a bar line.

Pentascale melody: C minor

Notes:	C	E♭	D	F	E♭		G	E♭	D	C
Count:	1	2	3	4	1 2 3 4	1	2	3	4	1 2 3 4

1. Name the Pentascale notes: C Major ___, ___, ___, ___, ___. C minor ___, ___, ___, ___, ___.

2. In $\frac{4}{4}$ Time, measures have notes and/or rests that equal 4 counts & are divided by a ____ _____.

3. Add bar lines to divide the rhythm into equal measures of four beats in each measure.
   For each melody: Name the notes. Write the counts below each measure. Play each melody.
   Name the Pentascale melody as: C Major or C minor.

Pentascale melody: ___ _____

Notes: ___ ___ ___ ___ ___ ___ ___ ___ ___ ___ ___ ___

Count: _____ _____ _____ _____

Pentascale melody: ___ _____

Notes: ___ ___ ___ ___ ___ ___ ___ ___ ___ ___

Count: _____ _____ _____ _____

PENTASCALE MELODIES - D MINOR (SAD) and D MAJOR (HAPPY)

A melody has different rest values (quarter = 1, half = 2, whole = 4) of silence indicated by a REST.

So-La Says: A melody may be written based on the 5 notes of the D minor or D Major Pentascale. In $\frac{4}{4}$ Time, each type of note/rest has a specific note/rest value. A quarter rest equals 1 count.

Pentascale melody: D minor   quarter rest   half rest   whole rest

Notes: D   A   G   F   E   F E D

Count: 1 2 3 4   1   2   3   4   1   2   3 4   1 2 3 4

1. Name the Pentascale notes: D minor ___, ___, ___, ___, ___. D Major ___, ___, ___, ___, ___.

2. In $\frac{4}{4}$ Time, rest values are: quarter rest = ___ beat, half rest = ___ beats, whole rest = ___ beats.

3. Add one rest (quarter, half or whole) below each bracket to indicate four beats in each measure. For each melody: Name the notes. Write the counts below each measure. Play each melody. Name the Pentascale melody as: D minor or D Major.

Pentascale melody: ___ _____

Notes: __ __ __   __ __ __   __ __

Count: _____   _____   _____

Pentascale melody: ___ _____

Notes: __ __ __ __ __ __   __ __ __

Count: _____   _____   _____   _____

PENTASCALE MELODIES - A MINOR (SAD) and A MAJOR (HAPPY)

A Pentascale melody moves by intervals and direction of notes to create sound called PATTERNS.

So-La Says: A melody may be written based on the 5 notes of the A minor or A Major Pentascale.

Melody notes have Patterns: same (1), step (2), skip (3), leap (5) and direction (up, down).

Pentascale melody: A Major

	step up	skip down	same line	leap down
Notes:	A B	C# A	B B C#	E A
Count:	1 2 3 4	1 2 3 4	1 2 3 4	1 2 3 4

1. Name the Pentascale notes: A minor ___, ___, ___, ___, ___. A Major ___, ___, ___, ___, ___.

2. Melody notes have Patterns: _____ (1), _____ (2), _____ (3), _____ (5) and direction.

3. Add one half note below each bracket to indicate the pattern and direction.
   For each melody: Name the notes. Write the counts below each measure. Play each melody.
   Name the Pentascale melody as: A minor or A Major.

Pentascale melody: ___ _____

Notes: ___ ___   ___ ___   ___ ___   ___ ___

Count: _____   _____   _____   _____

Pentascale melody: ___ _____

Notes: ___ ___   ___ ___   ___ ___   ___ ___ ___

Count: _____   _____   _____   _____

Lesson 11   Review with So-La & Ti-Do

Check:

1.   Identify each Musical Concept by filling in the blanks. Use the following words (terms):

    Bar Line   Time Signature   Whole Rest   Half Rest   Quarter Rest   Flat

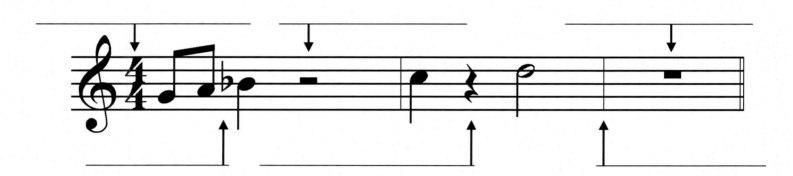

2.   Write the $\frac{4}{4}$ Time Signature at the beginning of each melody, after the Clef Sign.
     Add one rest (quarter, half or whole) below each bracket to complete each measure with 4 counts.
     Name the notes.
     Play each melody on the piano. Circle the correct answer to each question below.

Notes: ____   ____ ____ ____   ____

    a) This melody is in: D Major Pentascale   or   D minor Pentascale.

    b) This melody is played with the: Right Hand   or   Left Hand.

Notes: ____ ____ ____ ____   ____ ____ ____

    c) This melody is in: D Major Pentascale   or   D minor Pentascale.

    d) This melody is played with the: Right Hand   or   Left Hand.

Lesson 11 Review Ultimate Sight Reading & Ear Training Games

1. Play "Pillow Fight"!
    WRITE the counts below each measure.
    ADD one note below each bracket to indicate the pattern and direction. Use the correct note
     value (quarter note, half note or whole note) to complete each measure with 4 counts.

    Your Teacher will count out loud and play one melody . Listen to the melody and the rhythm.
    COLOR the correct Pillow.

Lesson 12   Analysis - Dynamics, Articulation & Tempo

DYNAMICS - FORTE, MEZZO FORTE, MEZZO PIANO, PIANO

Italian terms, symbols or signs are used to indicate how music is to be played.
DYNAMICS are signs that indicate the VOLUME (loud, medium loud, etc.) of sound.

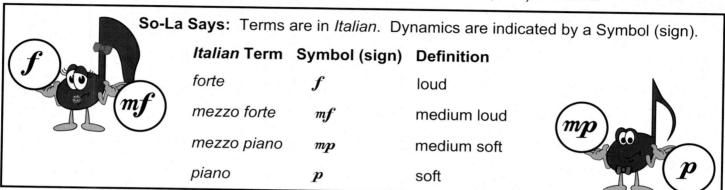

So-La Says: Terms are in *Italian*. Dynamics are indicated by a Symbol (sign).

Italian Term	Symbol (sign)	Definition
forte	*f*	loud
mezzo forte	*mf*	medium loud
mezzo piano	*mp*	medium soft
piano	*p*	soft

♫ **Ti-Do Tip:** Dynamics are written below the Treble Clef and are written above the Bass Clef.

1. Name the notes. Write the *Italian* term for the dynamic symbol. Write the definition of the term.
   Play each melody below. Use the given dynamics to play *forte, mezzo forte, mezzo piano or piano*.
   Name each Pentascale melody as: Major (C, D, G, A) or minor (C, D, G, A).

Pentascale melody: ___ _____

Pentascale melody: ___ _____

Notes: ___ ___ ___

Notes: ___ ___ ___ ___ ___ ___

Italian term: _____

Italian term: _____

Definition: _____

Definition: _____

Pentascale melody: ___ _____

Pentascale melody: ___ _____

Notes: ___ ___ ___ ___ ___ ___ ___ ___

Notes: ___ ___ ___ ___ ___ ___

Italian term: _____

Italian term: _____

Definition: _____

Definition: _____

ARTICULATION - LEGATO, (SMOOTH), STACCATO (DETACHED), FERMATA (PAUSE)

Italian Terms, symbols or signs are used in music to show expression in the melody.
ARTICULATION are signs that indicate the TOUCH (smooth, detached, pause), how notes are played.

So-La Says: *Italian* terms for Articulation are indicated by a Symbol (sign).

	Italian Term	Symbol (sign)	Definition
The Italian term *legato* means smooth. A smooth curved line called a slur is a sign to play the notes *legato* (smooth).	*legato* (slur)		smooth (play notes *legato*)
The Italian term *staccato* means detached. A dot above or below the notehead means to play the note sharply detached (not smooth).	*staccato* (dot)		detached (sharply detached)
The Italian term *fermata* means pause. A curved line and dot above the staff means to hold the note/rest longer than its written value.	*fermata* (curved line dot inside)	⌢·	pause (hold longer)

1. Name the notes. Write the *Italian* term for the articulation symbol. Write the definition of the term. Play each melody below. Use the given articulation to play *legato, staccato or fermata*. Name each Pentascale melody as: Major (C, D, G, A) or minor (C, D, G, A).

Pentascale melody: ___ _____

Notes: __ __ __ __ __ __ __ __

Italian term: _____

Definition: _____

Pentascale melody: ___ _____

Notes: __ __ __ __ __ __ __ __

Italian term: _____

Definition: _____

Pentascale melody: ___ _____

Notes: __ __ __ __ __ __ __

Italian term: _____

Definition: _____

Pentascale melody: ___ _____

Notes: __ __ __ __ __ __

Italian term: _____

Definition: _____

TEMPO - ALLEGRO (FAST), MODERATO (MODERATE) and LENTO (SLOW)

Italian Terms are used in music to show the rate of speed to play music.
TEMPO terms indicate the SPEED (slow, moderate or fast) at which the music is to be played.

So-La Says: *Italian* terms for Tempo are indicated by a Term written above the staff.

Tempo
↓
Allegro

Italian **Term**	**Definition**
Lento	slow
Moderato	moderate
Allegro	fast

♫ **Ti-Do Tip:** Tempo term is written once above the Time Signature at the top left of the music.

1. Name the notes. Write the *Italian* term for the tempo. Write the definition of the tempo term. Play each melody below. Use the given tempo to play *Lento, Moderato or Allegro*. Name each Pentascale melody as: Major (C, D, G, A) or minor (C, D, G, A).

Pentascale melody: ___ _____

Allegro

Notes: ___ ___ ___ ___ ___ ___ ___ ___

Italian term: _____

Definition: _____

Pentascale melody: ___ _____

Moderato

Notes: ___ ___ ___ ___ ___ ___ ___

Italian term: _____

Definition: _____

Pentascale melody: ___ _____

Lento

Notes: ___ ___ ___ ___ ___ ___

Italian term: _____

Definition: _____

Pentascale melody: ___ _____

Allegro

Notes: ___ ___ ___ ___ ___ ___

Italian term: _____

Definition: _____

ITALIAN TERMS and DEFINITIONS

Italian Terms, symbols or signs are musical terms used to show how the music is to be played.
The Composer (the person who wrote the music) uses *Italian* terms to indicate performance details.

So-La Says: *Italian* terms are indicated for Tempo - speed, Dynamics - volume, Articulation - touch.

Tempo	Definition	Dynamics	Definition	Articulation	Definition
Lento	slow	*forte*	loud	*legato*	smooth
Moderato	moderate	*mezzo forte*	medium loud	*staccato*	detached
Allegro	fast	*mezzo piano*	medium soft	*fermata*	pause
		piano	soft		

♫ **Ti-Do Tip:** *Italian* terms (signs) are indicated for Tempo, Dynamics and Articulation.

1. Write the *Italian* term for the Tempo, Dynamics and Articulation for each melody.
   Play each melody below. Use the given tempo, dynamics and articulation.
   Name each Pentascale melody as: Major (C, D, G, A) or minor (C, D, G, A).

Pentascale melody: ___ _____

Lento

Tempo: _____

Dynamics: _____

Articulation: _____

Pentascale melody: ___ _____

Allegro

Tempo: _____

Dynamics: _____

Articulation: _____

Pentascale melody: ___ _____

Moderato *f*

Tempo: _____

Dynamics: _____

Articulation: _____

Pentascale melody: ___ _____

Lento *mp*

Tempo: _____

Dynamics: _____

Articulation: _____

PENTASCALE MELODIES - MAJOR and MINOR - DYNAMICS, ARTICULATION and TEMPO

Pentascale Melodies (Major or minor) have patterns (same, step, skip, leap), direction (up, down), rhythm (note/rest values), tempo (speed), dynamics (volume) and articulation (touch).

 **So-La Says:** A Melody is the language of music used to tell a story, share a musical idea, or express a feeling.

Italian terms, symbols or signs are a "guide" in how to play the music.

1. Answer the questions below each melody. Play each melody (observe the terms, symbols & signs).

a) Name the note that is a flat: _____. Circle if the Pentascale melody is: Major or minor.

b) Name the Italian term for the tempo: fast _____.

c) Name the Italian terms for the articulation: smooth _____, detached _____.

d) Name the Italian term for the dynamics: medium loud _____.

e) Name the type of rest that equals 2 beats in $\frac{4}{4}$ time: _____ rest.

f) Name the last two notes: ____ and ____. Circle if the pattern is: leap up or leap down.

a) Name the note that is a sharp: _____. Circle if the Pentascale melody is: Major or minor.

b) Name the Italian term for the tempo: slow _____.

c) Name the Italian term for the articulation: pause, hold longer than written value _____.

d) Name the Italian term for the dynamics: medium soft _____.

e) Name the type of rest that equals 1 beat in $\frac{4}{4}$ time: _____ rest.

f) Name the last two notes: ____ and ____. Circle if the pattern is: skip up or skip down.

ANALYSIS and PLAYING MUSIC

So-La Says: ANALYSIS in music is like being a DETECTIVE.

Analysis is looking for clues in music. Analysis helps us learn how to read music faster and play music easier.

Be a detective. Look for the TOP 10 Clues!

♫ **Ti-Do Tip:** Read the question carefully. Use the Detective Clues to find the correct answer.

> **#1** Landmark: Treble Clef Middle C, G, C, High G. Bass Clef Middle C, F, C, Low F
>
> **#2** Pattern Numbers: Up or Down - same (1), step (2), skip (3), leap (5), octave (8)
>
> **#3** Note/Rest Values: Whole = 4 beats, Half = 2 beats, Quarter = 1 beat

1. Bass Clef landmark notes: Middle ____, Bass ____, Bass ____, Low ____.

2. In $\frac{4}{4}$ time: Half Rest = ____ beats and a Whole Rest = ____ beats.

3. Pattern interval numbers are: same (___), step (___), skip (___), leap (___), octave (___).

> **#4** Pentascales: Major (WS, WS, HS, WS) or minor (WS, HS, WS, WS)
>
> **#5** Accidental: Sharp raises a note one half step, Flat lowers a note one half step
>
> **#6** Natural sign: Cancels a Sharp or a Flat back to the original pitch (white key)

4. Pentascale pattern of steps: Major ___, ___, ___, ___, minor ___, ___, ___, ___.

5. To change Pentascale D minor to D Major, raise the third note F to _____.

6. To change Pentascale G Major to G minor, lower the third note B to _____.

> **#7** In $\frac{4}{4}$ Time Signature: Two eighth notes beamed together equal 1 beat
>
> **#8** Tempo: *Lento* (slow), *Moderato* (moderate), *Allegro* (fast)
>
> **#9** Articulation: *legato* (smooth), *staccato* (detached), *fermata* (pause)
>
> **#10** Dynamics: *forte* (loud), *mezzo forte* (medium loud), *mezzo piano* (medium soft), *piano* (soft)

7. In $\frac{4}{4}$ Time Signature, two eighth notes beamed together equal ___ beat.

8. The definition of the *Italian* term *mezzo forte* is _____.

9. *Italian* term for the sign meaning pause (hold longer than written value) is _____.

10. Definition of the tempo term: *Lento* _____, *Moderato* _____, *Allegro* _____.

Lesson 12   Review with So-La & Ti-Do

Check:

1. Match each Musical Term with the English Definition by writing the Definition Letter Name beside the Term. (Cross off each Definition Letter Name as it is used. All Definitions will only be used once.)

Musical Term		**English Definition**
Write the Definition Letter Name here. ↓		Cross off the Definition Letter Name after matching it to the Musical Term. ↓

Musical Term		English Definition
Dynamics	_____	a) The speed at which music is played.
Tempo	_a_	b) The touch, how notes are played.
Articulation	_____	c) The volume of the sound.
legato	_____	d) Articulation meaning to hold longer than the written value.
staccato	_____	e) Articulation meaning to play smooth.
fermata	_____	f) Articulation meaning to play detached.
Allegro	_____	g) Tempo meaning to play at a moderate speed.
Moderato	_____	h) Tempo meaning to play at a fast speed.
Lento	_____	i) Tempo meaning to play at a slow speed.
forte (f)	_____	j) Dynamic meaning to play soft.
mezzo forte (mf)	_____	k) Dynamic meaning to play medium soft.
mezzo piano (mp)	_____	l) Dynamic meaning to play medium loud.
piano (p)	_____	m) Dynamic meaning to play loud.

Lesson 12 Review Ultimate Sight Reading & Ear Training Games

1. LISTEN as your Teacher plays each song on the piano. For each measure, discuss the:
   PENTASCALE melody (D Major or D minor).
   PATTERN DIRECTION (same, step up, step down, skip up or skip down).
   ARTICULATION (legato, staccato or fermata).

2. With your Teacher, PLAY (on the piano) each melody. Count out loud.

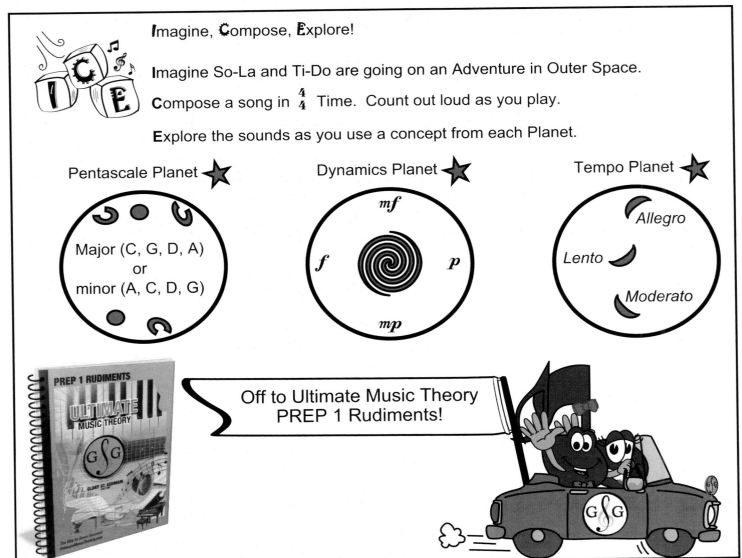

Imagine, Compose, Explore!

Imagine So-La and Ti-Do are going on an Adventure in Outer Space.

Compose a song in $\frac{4}{4}$ Time. Count out loud as you play.

Explore the sounds as you use a concept from each Planet.

Pentascale Planet

Major (C, G, D, A)
or
minor (A, C, D, G)

Dynamics Planet

mf
f   *p*
mp

Tempo Planet

Allegro
Lento
Moderato

Off to Ultimate Music Theory
PREP 1 Rudiments!

PREP 1 RUDIMENTS
ULTIMATE MUSIC THEORY

Ultimate Music Theory Certificate

_____

has successfully completed all the requirements of the

Music Theory Beginner C

_____   _____

Music Teacher   *Date*

Enriching Lives Through Music Education